THE HISTORY OF THE CHURCH

FROM CHRIST TO CONSTANTINE

VOLUME ONE OF TWO

GRAND TYPE
GRANDTYPECLASSICS.COM

The History of the Church
From Christ to Constantine
Eusebius c.260 – c.340
Translated by Arthur Cushman McGiffert
Translation published by T. & T. Clark in 1890
McGiffert, Arthur Cushman 1861 – 1933

ISBN: 978-1-83412-412-4 Volume One
ISBN: 978-1-83412-413-1 Volume Two

THE HISTORY OF THE CHURCH

FROM CHRIST TO CONSTANTINE

VOLUME ONE OF TWO

EUSEBIUS

Translated by
Arthur Cushman McGiffert

GRAND TYPE CLASSICS

CONTENTS

Book Two

VOLUME TWO

Book Six

Book Seven

Book Eight

BOOK ONE

CHAPTER ONE

The Plan of the Work

1. IT IS MY PURPOSE to write an account of the lines of succession of the holy apostles, as well as of the times that have elapsed from the days of our Saviour to our own; and to relate the many important

events that are said to have occurred in the history of the Church; and to mention those who have governed and presided over the Church in the most prominent parishes, and those who in each generation have proclaimed the divine word either orally or in writing.

2. It is my purpose also to give the names and number and dates of those who through love of innovation have run into the greatest errors, and, proclaiming themselves discoverers of knowledge falsely so-called 1 Timothy 6:20 have like fierce wolves mercilessly devastated the flock of Christ.

3. It is my intention, moreover, to recount the misfortunes that immediately came upon the whole Jewish nation in consequence of their plots against our Saviour, and to record the ways and the times in which the divine word has been attacked by the Gentiles, and to describe the character of those who at various periods have contended for it in

the face of blood and of tortures, as well as the confessions which have been made in our own days, and finally the gracious and kindly succor which our Saviour has afforded them all. Since I propose to write of all these things I shall commence my work with the beginning of the dispensation [οἰκονομία] of our Saviour and Lord Jesus Christ. [Several manuscripts, editors and translators read τοῦ θεοῦ after χριστόν. But the best manuscripts and sources, included Rufinus, omit τοῦ θεοῦ.]

4. But at the outset I must crave for my work the indulgence of the wise, for I confess that it is beyond my power to produce a perfect and complete history, and since I am the first to enter upon the subject, I am attempting to traverse as it were a lonely and untrodden path. I pray that I may have God as my guide and the power of the Lord as my aid, since I am unable to find even the bare footsteps of those who have traveled the way before me, except in brief fragments, in which

some in one way, others in another, have transmitted to us particular accounts of the times in which they lived. From afar they raise their voices like torches, and they cry out, as from some lofty and conspicuous watchtower, admonishing us where to walk and how to direct the course of our work steadily and safely.

5. Having gathered therefore from the matters mentioned here and there by them whatever we consider important for the present work, and having plucked like flowers from a meadow the appropriate passages from ancient writers, we shall endeavor to embody the whole in a historical narrative, content if we preserve the memory of the lines of succession of the apostles of our Saviour; if not indeed of all, yet of the most renowned of them in those churches that are the most noted, and which even to the present time are held in honor.

6. This work seems especially important to me because I know of no ecclesiastical

writer who has devoted himself to this subject. I hope that it will appear most useful to those who are fond of historical research.

7. I have already given a summary of these things in the Chronological Canons that I have composed, but notwithstanding that, I have undertaken in the present work to write as full an account of them as I am able.

8. My work will begin, as I have said, with the dispensation [οἰκονομία] of the Saviour Christ – which is loftier and greater than human conception – and with a discussion of his divinity.

9. For it is necessary, inasmuch as we derive even our name from Christ, for one who proposes to write a history of the Church to begin with the very origin of Christ's dispensation, a dispensation more divine than many think.

CHAPTER TWO

Summary View of the Pre-existence and Divinity of Our Saviour and Lord Jesus Christ

1. SINCE IN CHRIST there is a twofold nature, and the one – in so far as he is thought of as God – resembles the head of the body, while the other may be compared with the feet – in so far as he, for the sake

of our salvation, put on human nature with the same passions as our own – the following work will be complete only if we begin with the chief and lordliest events of all his history. In this way will the antiquity and divinity of Christianity be shown to those who suppose it of recent and foreign origin, [νέαν αὐτὴν καὶ ἐκτετοπισμένην] and imagine that it appeared only yesterday. [This was one of the principal objections raised against Christianity. A religion could not be considered true unless it had ancient origins. Hence the Church Fathers laid great stress upon the antiquity of Christianity, and emphasized the Old Testament as a Christian book.]

2. No language is sufficient to express the origin and the worth, the being and the nature of Christ. Wherefore also the Holy Spirit says in the prophecies, **"Who shall declare his generation?"** Isaiah 53:8 For none knows the Father except the Son, neither can any one know the Son adequately except the

Father alone who has begotten him.

3. For who beside the Father could clearly understand the Light which was before the world, the intellectual and essential Wisdom which existed before the ages, the living Word which was in the beginning with the Father and which was God, the first and only begotten of God which was before every creature and creation visible and invisible, the commander-in-chief of the rational and immortal host of heaven, the messenger of the great counsel, the executor of the Father's unspoken will, the creator, with the Father, of all things, the second cause of the universe after the Father, the true and only-begotten Son of God, the Lord and God and King of all created things, the one who has received dominion and power, with divinity itself, and with might and honor from the Father; as it is said in regard to him in the mystical passages of Scripture which speak of his divinity: **"In the beginning was the Word,**

and the Word was with God, and the Word was God." John 1:1 "**All things were made by him; and without him was not anything made.**" John 1:3

4. This, too, the great Moses teaches, when, as the most ancient of all the prophets, he describes under the influence of the divine Spirit the creation and arrangement of the universe. He declares that the maker of the world and the creator of all things yielded to Christ himself, and to none other than his own clearly divine and firstborn Word, the making of inferior things, and communed with him respecting the creation of man. "**For,**" says he, "**God said, Let us make man in our image and in our likeness.**" Genesis 1:26

5. And another of the prophets confirms this, speaking of God in his hymns as follows: "**He spoke and they were made; he commanded and they were created.**" He here introduces the Father and Maker as Ruler of all, commanding with a kingly nod,

and second to him the divine Word, none other than the one who is proclaimed by us, as carrying out the Father's commands.

6. All that are said to have excelled in righteousness and piety since the creation of man, the great servant Moses and before him in the first place Abraham and his children, and as many righteous men and prophets as afterward appeared, have contemplated him with the pure eyes of the mind, and have recognized him and offered to him the worship which is due him as Son of God.

7. But he, by no means neglectful of the reverence due to the Father, was appointed to teach the knowledge of the Father to them all. For instance, the Lord God, it is said, appeared as a common man to Abraham while he was sitting at the oak of Mambre. And he, immediately falling down, although he saw a man with his eyes, nevertheless worshipped him as God, and sacrificed to him as Lord, and confessed that he was not

ignorant of his identity when he uttered the words, **"Lord, the judge of all the earth, will you not execute righteous judgment?"** Genesis 18:25

8. For if it is unreasonable to suppose that the unbegotten and immutable essence of the almighty God was changed into the form of man or that it deceived the eyes of the beholders with the appearance of some created thing, and if it is unreasonable to suppose, on the other hand, that the Scripture should falsely invent such things, when the God and Lord who judges all the earth and executes judgment is seen in the form of a man, who else can be called, if it be not lawful to call him the first cause of all things, than his only pre-existent Word? [Eusebius accepts the common view of the early Church, that the theophanies of the Old Testament were Christophanies; that is, appearances of the second person of the Trinity. Augustine seems to have been the first of the Fathers to take a different

view, maintaining that such Christophanies were not consistent with the identity of essence between Father and Son, and that the Scriptures themselves teach that it was not the Logos, but an angel, that appeared to the Old Testament worthies on various occasions (cf. On the Trinity III.11). Augustine's opinion was widely adopted, but in modern times the earlier view, which Eusebius represents, has been the prevailing one.] Concerning whom it is said in the Psalms, **"He sent his Word and healed them, and delivered them from their destructions."** Psalm 107:20

9. Moses most clearly proclaims him second Lord after the Father, when he says, **"The Lord rained upon Sodom and Gomorrha brimstone and fire from the Lord."** Genesis 19:24 The divine Scripture also calls him God, when he appeared again to Jacob in the form of a man, and said to Jacob, **"Your name shall be called no more Jacob, but**

Israel shall be your name, because you have prevailed with God." Genesis 32:28 Wherefore also Jacob called that place Vision of God [εἶδος θεοῦ] – saying, "**For I have seen God face to face, and my life is preserved.**" Genesis 32:30

10. Nor is it admissible to suppose that the theophanies recorded were appearances of subordinate angels and ministers of God, for whenever any of these appeared to men, the Scripture does not conceal the fact, but calls them by name not **God** nor **Lord**, but **angels**, as it is easy to prove by numberless testimonies.

11. Joshua, also, the successor of Moses, calls him, as leader of the heavenly angels and archangels and of the supramundane powers, and as lieutenant of the Father, entrusted with the second rank of sovereignty and rule over all, "**captain of the host of the Lord,**" although he saw him not otherwise than again in the form and appearance of a man. For it is written:

12. "**And it came to pass when Joshua was** at Jericho [ἐν Ἱεριχῶ] **that he looked and saw a man standing over against him with his sword drawn in his hand, and Joshua went unto him and said, Are you for us or for our adversaries? And he said to him, As captain of the host of the Lord am I now come. And Joshua fell on his face to the earth and said to him, Lord, what do you command your servant? And the captain of the Lord said to Joshua, Loose your shoe from off your feet, for the place whereon you stand is holy.**"

13. You will perceive also from the same words that this was no other than he who talked with Moses. For the Scripture says in the same words and with reference to the same one, "**When the Lord saw that he drew near to see, the Lord called to him out of the bush and said, Moses, Moses. And he said, What is it? And he said, Draw not near hither; loose your shoe from**

off your feet, for the place whereon you stand is holy ground. And he said to him, I am the God of your fathers, the God of Abraham, and the God of Isaac, and the God of Jacob."

14. And that there is a certain substance which lived and subsisted before the world, and which ministered unto the Father and God of the universe for the formation of all created things, and which is called the Word of God and Wisdom, we may learn, to quote other proofs in addition to those already cited, from the mouth of Wisdom herself, who reveals most clearly through Solomon the following mysteries concerning herself: **"I, Wisdom, have dwelt with prudence and knowledge, and I have invoked understanding. Through me kings reign, and princes ordain righteousness. Through me the great are magnified, and through me sovereigns rule the earth."**

15. To which she adds: **"The Lord created**

me in the beginning of his ways, for his works; before the world he established me, in the beginning, before he made the earth, before he made the depths, before the mountains were settled, before all hills he begot me. When he prepared the heavens I was present with him, and when he established the fountains of the region under heaven I was with him, disposing. I was the one in whom he delighted; daily I rejoiced before him at all times when he was rejoicing at having completed the world."

16. That the divine Word, therefore, pre-existed and appeared to some, if not to all, has thus been briefly shown by us.

17. But why the Gospel was not preached in ancient times to all men and to all nations, as it is now, will appear from the following considerations. The life of the ancients was not of such a kind as to permit them to receive the all-wise and all-virtuous teaching of Christ.

18. For immediately in the beginning, after his original life of blessedness, the first man despised the command of God, and fell into this mortal and perishable state, and exchanged his former divinely inspired luxury for this curse-laden earth. His descendants having filled our earth, showed themselves much worse, with the exception of one here and there, and entered upon a certain brutal and insupportable mode of life.

19. They thought neither of city nor state, neither of arts nor sciences. They were ignorant even of the name of laws and of justice, of virtue and of philosophy. As nomads, they passed their lives in deserts, like wild and fierce beasts, destroying, by an excess of voluntary wickedness, the natural reason of man, and the seeds of thought and of culture implanted in the human soul. They gave themselves wholly over to all kinds of profanity, now seducing one another, now slaying one another, now eating human flesh,

and now daring to wage war with the Gods and to undertake those battles of the giants celebrated by all; now planning to fortify earth against heaven, and in the madness of ungoverned pride to prepare an attack upon the very God of all.

20. On account of these things, when they conducted themselves thus, the all-seeing God sent down upon them floods and conflagrations as upon a wild forest spread over the whole earth. He cut them down with continuous famines and plagues, with wars, and with thunderbolts from heaven, as if to check some terrible and obstinate disease of souls with more severe punishments.

21. Then, when the excess of wickedness had overwhelmed nearly all the race, like a deep fit of drunkenness, beclouding and darkening the minds of men, the first-born and first-created wisdom of God, the pre-existent Word himself, induced by his exceeding love for man, appeared to his servants, now in the form of angels, and again to one and another

of those ancients who enjoyed the favor of God, in his own person as the saving power of God, not otherwise, however, than in the shape of man, because it was impossible to appear in any other way.

22. And as by them the seeds of piety were sown among a multitude of men and the whole nation, descended from the Hebrews, devoted themselves persistently to the worship of God, he imparted to them through the prophet Moses, as to multitudes still corrupted by their ancient practices, images and symbols of a certain mystic Sabbath and of circumcision, and elements of other spiritual principles, but he did not grant them a complete knowledge of the mysteries themselves.

23. But when their law became celebrated, and, like a sweet odor, was diffused among all men, as a result of their influence the dispositions of the majority of the heathen were softened by the lawgivers and philosophers who arose on every side, and

their wild and savage brutality was changed into mildness, so that they enjoyed deep peace, friendship, and social intercourse. Then, finally, at the time of the origin of the Roman Empire, there appeared again to all men and nations throughout the world, who had been, as it were, previously assisted, and were now fitted to receive the knowledge of the Father, that same teacher of virtue, the minister of the Father in all good things, the divine and heavenly Word of God, in a human body not at all differing in substance from our own. He did and suffered the things which had been prophesied. For it had been foretold that one who was at the same time man and God should come and dwell in the world, should perform wonderful works, and should show himself a teacher to all nations of the piety of the Father. The marvelous nature of his birth, and his new teaching, and his wonderful works had also been foretold; so likewise the manner of his death, his resurrection from the dead, and, finally, his divine ascension into heaven.

24. For instance, Daniel the prophet, under the influence of the divine Spirit, seeing his kingdom at the end of time, was inspired thus to describe the divine vision in language fitted to human comprehension: **"For I beheld,"** he says, **"until thrones were placed, and the Ancient of Days did sit, whose garment was white as snow and the hair of his head like pure wool; his throne was a flame of fire and his wheels burning fire. A river of fire flowed before him. Thousand thousands ministered unto him, and ten thousand times ten thousand stood before him. He appointed judgment, and the books were opened."** Daniel 7:9-10

25. And again, **"I saw,"** says he, **"and beheld, one like the Son of man came with the clouds of heaven, and he hastened unto the Ancient of Days and was brought into his presence, and there was given him the dominion and the glory**

and the kingdom; and all peoples, tribes, and tongues serve him. His dominion is an everlasting dominion which shall not pass away, and his kingdom shall not be destroyed." Daniel 7:13-14

26. It is clear that these words can refer to no one else than to our Saviour, the God Word who was in the beginning with God, and who was called the Son of man because of his final appearance in the flesh.

27. But since we have collected in separate books the selections from the prophets which relate to our Saviour Jesus Christ, and have arranged in a more logical form those things which have been revealed concerning him, what has been said will suffice for the present.

CHAPTER THREE

The Name Jesus and also the Name Christ were known from the Beginning, and were honored by the Inspired Prophets

1. IT IS NOW THE proper place to show that the very name Jesus and also the name Christ were honored by the ancient prophets beloved of God.

53

2. Moses was the first to make known the name of Christ as a name especially august and glorious. When he delivered types and symbols of heavenly things, and mysterious images, in accordance with the oracle which said to him, **"Look that you make all things according to the pattern which was shown you in the mount,"** Exodus 25:40 he consecrated a man high priest of God, in so far as that was possible, and him he called **Christ**. And thus to this dignity of the high priesthood, which in his opinion surpassed the most honorable position among men, he attached for the sake of honor and glory the name of Christ.

3. He knew so well that in **Christ** was something divine. And the same one foreseeing, under the influence of the divine Spirit, the name Jesus, dignified it also with a certain distinguished privilege. For the name of Jesus, which had never been uttered among men before the time of Moses, he applied first and only to the

one who he knew would receive after his death, again as a type and symbol, the supreme command.

4. His successor, therefore, who had not hitherto borne the name Jesus, but had been called by another name, Auses, which had been given him by his parents, he now called Jesus, bestowing the name upon him as a gift of honor, far greater than any kingly diadem. For Jesus himself, the son of Nave, bore a resemblance to our Saviour in the fact that he alone, after Moses and after the completion of the symbolic worship which had been transmitted by him, succeeded to the government of the true and pure religion.

5. Thus Moses bestowed the name of our Saviour, Jesus Christ, as a mark of the highest honor, upon the two men who in his time surpassed all the rest of the people in virtue and glory; namely, upon the high priest and upon his own successor in the government.

6. And the prophets that came after also

clearly foretold Christ by name, predicting at the same time the plots which the Jewish people would form against him, and the calling of the nations through him. Jeremiah, for instance, speaks as follows: **"The Spirit before our face, Christ the Lord, was taken in their destructions; of whom we said, under his shadow we shall live among the nations."** Lamentations 4:20 And David, in perplexity, says, **"Why did the nations rage and the people imagine vain things? The kings of the earth set themselves in array, and the rulers were gathered together against the Lord and against his Christ"**; to which he adds, in the person of Christ himself, **"The Lord said to me, You are my Son, this day have I begotten you. Ask of me, and I will give you the nations for your inheritance, and the uttermost parts of the earth for your possession."**

7. And not only those who were honored with the high priesthood, and who for the

sake of the symbol were anointed with especially prepared oil, were adorned with the name of Christ among the Hebrews, but also the kings whom the prophets anointed under the influence of the divine Spirit, and thus constituted, as it were, typical Christs. For they also bore in their own persons types of the royal and sovereign power of the true and only Christ, the divine Word who rules over all.

8. And we have been told also that certain of the prophets themselves became, by the act of anointing, Christs in type, so that all these have reference to the true Christ, the divinely inspired and heavenly Word, who is the only high priest of all, and the only King of every creature, and the Father's only supreme prophet of prophets.

9. And a proof of this is that no one of those who were of old symbolically anointed, whether priests, or kings, or prophets, possessed so great a power of inspired virtue as was exhibited by our Saviour and

Lord Jesus, the true and only Christ.

10. None of them at least, however superior in dignity and honor they may have been for many generations among their own people, ever gave to their followers the name of **Christians** from their own typical name of **Christ**. Neither was divine honor ever rendered to any one of them by their subjects; nor after their death was the disposition of their followers such that they were ready to die for the one whom they honored. And never did so great a commotion arise among all the nations of the earth in respect to any one of that age; for the mere symbol could not act with such power among them as the truth itself which was exhibited by our Saviour.

11. He, although he received no symbols and types of high priesthood from any one, although he was not born of a race of priests, although he was not elevated to a kingdom by military guards, although he was not a prophet like those of old, although he

obtained no honor nor pre-eminence among the Jews, nevertheless was adorned by the Father with all, if not with the symbols, yet with the truth itself.

12. And therefore, although he did not possess like honors with those whom we have mentioned, he is called **Christ** more than all of them. And as himself the true and only Christ of God, he has filled the whole earth with the truly august and sacred name of **Christians**, committing to his followers no longer types and images, but the uncovered virtues themselves, and a heavenly life in the very doctrines of truth.

13. And he was not anointed with oil prepared from material substances, but, as befits divinity, with the divine Spirit himself, by participation in the unbegotten deity of the Father. And this is taught also again by Isaiah, who exclaims, as if in the person of Christ himself, **"The Spirit of the Lord is upon me; therefore has he anointed me. He has sent me to preach the Gospel**

to the poor, to proclaim deliverance to captives, and recovery of sight to the blind."

14. And not only Isaiah, but also David addresses him, saying, **"Your throne, O God, is forever and ever. A scepter of equity is the scepter of your kingdom. You have loved righteousness and have hated iniquity. Therefore God, your God, has anointed you with the oil of gladness above your fellows."** Here the Scripture calls him God in the first verse, in the second it honors him with a royal scepter.

15. Then a little farther on, after the divine and royal power, it represents him in the third place as having become Christ, being anointed not with oil made of material substances, but with the divine oil of gladness. It thus indicates his special honor, far superior to and different from that of those who, as types, were of old anointed in a more material way.

16. And elsewhere the same writer speaks

of him as follows: **"The Lord said to my Lord, Sit at my right hand until I make your enemies your footstool"**; and, **"Out of the womb, before the morning star, have I begotten you. The Lord has sworn and he will not repent. You are a priest forever after the order of Melchizedek."**

17. But this Melchizedek is introduced in the Holy Scriptures as a priest of the most high God, not consecrated by any anointing oil, especially prepared, and not even belonging by descent to the priesthood of the Jews. Wherefore after his order, but not after the order of the others, who received symbols and types, was our Saviour proclaimed, with an appeal to an oath, Christ and priest.

18. History, therefore, does not relate that he was anointed corporeally by the Jews, nor that he belonged to the lineage of priests, but that he came into existence from God himself before the morning star, that is before the organization of the world, and that he obtained an immortal and

undecaying priesthood for eternal ages.

19. But it is a great and convincing proof of his incorporeal and divine unction that he alone of all those who have ever existed is even to the present day called Christ by all men throughout the world, and is confessed and witnessed to under this name, and is commemorated both by Greeks and Barbarians and even to this day is honored as a King by his followers throughout the world, and is admired as more than a prophet, and is glorified as the true and only high priest of God. And besides all this, as the pre-existent Word of God, called into being before all ages, he has received august honor from the Father, and is worshipped as God.

20. But most wonderful of all is the fact that we who have consecrated ourselves to him, honor him not only with our voices and with the sound of words, but also with complete elevation of soul, so that we choose to give testimony unto him rather

than to preserve our own lives.

21. I have of necessity prefaced my history with these matters in order that no one, judging from the date of his incarnation, may think that our Saviour and Lord Jesus, the Christ, has but recently come into being.

CHAPTER FOUR

The Religion Proclaimed by him to All Nations was Neither New Nor Strange

1. BUT THAT NO ONE may suppose that his doctrine is new and strange, as if it were framed by a man of recent origin, differing in no respect from other men, let us now briefly consider this point also.

2. It is admitted that when in recent times

the appearance of our Saviour Jesus Christ had become known to all men there immediately made its appearance a new nation; a nation confessedly not small, and not dwelling in some corner of the earth, but the most numerous and pious of all nations, indestructible and unconquerable, because it always receives assistance from God. This nation, thus suddenly appearing at the time appointed by the inscrutable counsel of God, is the one which has been honored by all with the name of Christ.

3. One of the prophets, when he saw beforehand with the eye of the Divine Spirit that which was to be, was so astonished at it that he cried out, **"Who has heard of such things, and who has spoken thus? Hath the earth brought forth in one day, and has a nation been born at once?"** Isaiah 66:8 And the same prophet gives a hint also of the name by which the nation was to be called, when he says, **"Those that serve me shall be called by a new**

name, which shall be blessed upon the earth." Isaiah 65:15-16

4. But although it is clear that we are new and that this new name of Christians has really but recently been known among all nations, nevertheless our life and our conduct, with our doctrines of religion, have not been lately invented by us, but from the first creation of man, so to speak, have been established by the natural understanding of divinely favored men of old. That this is so we shall show in the following way.

5. That the Hebrew nation is not new, but is universally honored on account of its antiquity, is known to all. The books and writings of this people contain accounts of ancient men, rare indeed and few in number, but nevertheless distinguished for piety and righteousness and every other virtue. Of these, some excellent men lived before the flood, others of the sons and descendants of Noah lived after it, among them Abraham, whom the Hebrews celebrate as their own

founder and forefather.

6. If any one should assert that all those who have enjoyed the testimony of righteousness, from Abraham himself back to the first man, were Christians in fact if not in name, he would not go beyond the truth.

7. For that which the name indicates, that the Christian man, through the knowledge and the teaching of Christ, is distinguished for temperance and righteousness, for patience in life and manly virtue, and for a profession of piety toward the one and only God over all – all that was zealously practiced by them not less than by us.

8. They did not care about circumcision of the body, neither do we. They did not care about observing Sabbaths, nor do we. They did not avoid certain kinds of food, neither did they regard the other distinctions which Moses first delivered to their posterity to be observed as symbols; nor do Christians of the present day do such things. But they

also clearly knew the very Christ of God; for it has already been shown that he appeared unto Abraham, that he imparted revelations to Isaac, that he talked with Jacob, that he held converse with Moses and with the prophets that came after.

9. Hence you will find those divinely favored men honored with the name of Christ, according to the passage which says of them, **"Touch not my Christs, and do my prophets no harm."**

10. So that it is clearly necessary to consider that religion, which has lately been preached to all nations through the teaching of Christ, the first and most ancient of all religions, and the one discovered by those divinely favored men in the age of Abraham.

11. If it is said that Abraham, a long time afterward, was given the command of circumcision, we reply that nevertheless before this it was declared that he had received the testimony of righteousness through faith; as the divine word says,

"Abraham believed in God, and it was counted unto him for righteousness." Genesis 15:6

12. And indeed unto Abraham, who was thus before his circumcision a justified man, there was given by God, who revealed himself unto him (but this was Christ himself, the word of God), a prophecy in regard to those who in coming ages should be justified in the same way as he. The prophecy was in the following words: **"And in you shall all the tribes of the earth be blessed."** Genesis 12:3 And again, **"He shall become a nation great and numerous; and in him shall all the nations of the earth be blessed."** Genesis 18:18

13. It is permissible to understand this as fulfilled in us. For he, having renounced the superstition of his fathers, and the former error of his life, and having confessed the one God over all, and having worshipped him with deeds of virtue, and not with the service of the law which was afterward

given by Moses, was justified by faith in Christ, the Word of God, who appeared unto him. To him, then, who was a man of this character, it was said that all the tribes and all the nations of the earth should be blessed in him.

14. But that very religion of Abraham has reappeared at the present time, practiced in deeds, more efficacious than words, by Christians alone throughout the world.

15. What then should prevent the confession that we who are of Christ practice one and the same mode of life and have one and the same religion as those divinely favored men of old? Whence it is evident that the perfect religion committed to us by the teaching of Christ is not new and strange, but, if the truth must be spoken, it is the first and the true religion. This may suffice for this subject.

CHAPTER FIVE

The Time of his Appearance among Men

1. AND NOW, after this necessary introduction to our proposed history of the Church, we can enter, so to speak, upon our journey, beginning with the appearance of our Saviour in the flesh. And we invoke God, the Father of the Word, and him, of whom we have been speaking, Jesus Christ

himself our Saviour and Lord, the heavenly Word of God, as our aid and fellow-laborer in the narration of the truth.

2. It was in the forty-second year of the reign of Augustus and the twenty-eighth after the subjugation of Egypt and the death of Antony and Cleopatra, with whom the dynasty of the Ptolemies in Egypt came to an end, that our Saviour and Lord Jesus Christ was born in Bethlehem of Judea, according to the prophecies which had been uttered concerning him. Micah 5:2 His birth took place during the first census, while Cyrenius was governor of Syria.

3. Flavius Josephus, the most celebrated of Hebrew historians, also mentions this census, which was taken during Cyrenius' term of office. In the same connection he gives an account of the uprising of the Galileans, which took place at that time, of which also Luke, among our writers, has made mention in the Acts, in the following words: **"After this man rose up Judas**

of Galilee in the days of the taxing, and drew away a multitude after him: he also perished; and all, even as many as obeyed him, were dispersed." Acts 5:37

4. The above-mentioned author, in the eighteenth book of his Antiquities, in agreement with these words, adds the following, which we quote exactly: "Cyrenius, a member of the senate, one who had held other offices and had passed through them all to the consulship, a man also of great dignity in other respects, came to Syria with a small retinue, being sent by Cæsar to be a judge of the nation and to make an assessment of their property."

5. And after a little he says: "But Judas, a Gaulonite, from a city called Gamala, taking with him Sadduchus, a Pharisee, urged the people to revolt, both of them saying that the taxation meant nothing else than downright slavery, and exhorting the nation to defend their liberty."

6. And in the second book of his History of the Jewish War, he writes as follows concerning the same man: **"At this time a certain Galilean, whose name was Judas, persuaded his countrymen to revolt, declaring that they were cowards if they submitted to pay tribute to the Romans, and if they endured, besides God, masters who were mortal."** These things are recorded by Josephus.

About the Time of Christ, in accordance with Prophecy, the Rulers who had governed the Jewish Nation in Regular Succession from the Days of Antiquity came to an End, and Herod, the First Foreigner, Became King

1. WHEN HEROD, the first ruler of foreign blood, became King, the prophecy of Moses received its fulfillment, according to which there should **"not be wanting a prince of Judah, nor a ruler from his loins, until he come for whom it is reserved."** The latter, he also shows, was to be the expectation of the nations.

2. This prediction remained unfulfilled so long as it was permitted them to live under rulers from their own nation, that is, from the time of Moses to the reign of Augustus. Under the latter, Herod, the first foreigner, was given the Kingdom of the Jews by the Romans. As Josephus relates, he was an Idumean on his father's side and an Arabian on his mother's. But Africanus, who was also no common writer, says that they who were more accurately informed about him report that he was a son of Antipater, and that the latter was the son of a certain Herod of Ascalon, one of the so-called servants of the temple of Apollo.

3. This Antipater, having been taken a prisoner while a boy by Idumean robbers, lived with them, because his father, being a poor man, was unable to pay a ransom for him. Growing up in their practices he was afterward befriended by Hyrcanus, the high priest of the Jews. A son of his was that Herod who lived in the times of our Saviour.

4. When the Kingdom of the Jews had devolved upon such a man the expectation of the nations was, according to prophecy, already at the door. For with him their princes and governors, who had ruled in regular succession from the time of Moses came to an end.

5. Before their captivity and their transportation to Babylon they were ruled by Saul first and then by David, and before the kings leaders governed them who were called Judges, and who came after Moses and his successor Jesus.

6. After their return from Babylon they continued to have without interruption an

aristocratic form of government, with an oligarchy. For the priests had the direction of affairs until Pompey, the Roman general, took Jerusalem by force, and defiled the holy places by entering the very innermost sanctuary of the temple. Aristobulus, who, by the right of ancient succession, had been up to that time both king and high priest, he sent with his children in chains to Rome; and gave to Hyrcanus, brother of Aristobulus, the high priesthood, while the whole nation of the Jews was made tributary to the Romans from that time.

7. But Hyrcanus, who was the last of the regular line of high priests, was very soon afterward taken prisoner by the Parthians, and Herod, the first foreigner, as I have already said, was made King of the Jewish nation by the Roman senate and by Augustus.

8. Under him Christ appeared in bodily shape, and the expected Salvation of the nations and their calling followed in

accordance with prophecy. From this time the princes and rulers of Judah, I mean of the Jewish nation, came to an end, and as a natural consequence the order of the high priesthood, which from ancient times had proceeded regularly in closest succession from generation to generation, was immediately thrown into confusion. [Eusebius' statement is perfectly correct. The high priestly lineage had been kept with great scrupulousness until Hyrcanus II, the last of the regular succession. (His grandson Aristobulus, however, was high priest for a year under Herod, but was then slain by him.) Afterward the high priest was appointed and changed at pleasure by the secular ruler. Herod the Great first established the practice of removing a high priest during his lifetime; and under him there were no less than six different ones.]

9. Of these things Josephus is also a witness, who shows that when Herod was made King by the Romans he no longer

appointed the high priests from the ancient line, but gave the honor to certain obscure persons. A course similar to that of Herod in the appointment of the priests was pursued by his son Archelaus, and after him by the Romans, who took the government into their own hands.

10. The same writer shows that Herod was the first that locked up the sacred garment of the high priest under his own seal and refused to permit the high priests to keep it for themselves. The same course was followed by Archelaus after him, and after Archelaus by the Romans.

11. These things have been recorded by us in order to show that another prophecy has been fulfilled in the appearance of our Saviour Jesus Christ. For the Scripture, in the Book of Daniel, Daniel 9:26 having expressly mentioned a certain number of weeks until the coming of Christ, of which we have treated in other books, most clearly prophesies, that after the completion of those

weeks the unction among the Jews should totally perish. And this, it has been clearly shown, was fulfilled at the time of the birth of our Saviour Jesus Christ. This has been necessarily premised by us as a proof of the correctness of the time.

CHAPTER SEVEN

The Alleged Discrepancy in the Gospels in regard to the Genealogy of Christ

1. MATTHEW AND LUKE IN their gospels have given us the genealogy of Christ differently, and many suppose that they are at variance with one another. Since as a consequence every believer, in ignorance of the truth, has been zealous to invent some

explanation which shall harmonize the two passages, permit us to subjoin the account of the matter which has come down to us, and which is given by Africanus, who was mentioned by us just above, in his epistle to Aristides, where he discusses the harmony of the gospel genealogies. After refuting the opinions of others as forced and deceptive, he give the account which he had received from tradition in these words:

2. For whereas the names of the generations were reckoned in Israel either according to nature or according to law – according to nature by the succession of legitimate offspring, and according to law whenever another raised up a child to the name of a brother dying childless; for because a clear hope of resurrection was not yet given they had a representation of the future promise by a kind of mortal resurrection, in order that the name of the one deceased might be perpetuated –

3. whereas then some of those who

are inserted in this genealogical table succeeded by natural descent, the son to the father, while others, though born of one father, were ascribed by name to another, mention was made of both of those who were progenitors in fact and of those who were so only in name.

4. Thus neither of the gospels is in error, for one reckons by nature, the other by law. For the line of descent from Solomon and that from Nathan were so involved, the one with the other, by the raising up of children to the childless and by second marriages, that the same persons are justly considered to belong at one time to one, at another time to another; that is, at one time to the reputed fathers, at another to the actual fathers. So that both these accounts are strictly true and come down to Joseph with considerable intricacy indeed, yet quite accurately.

5. But in order that what I have said may be made clear I shall explain the interchange of the generations. If we reckon the

generations from David through Solomon, the third from the end is found to be Matthan, who begot Jacob the father of Joseph. But if, with Luke, we reckon them from Nathan the son of David, in like manner the third from the end is Melchi, whose son Eli was the father of Joseph. For Joseph was the son of Eli, the son of Melchi.

6. Joseph therefore being the object proposed to us, it must be shown how it is that each is recorded to be his father, both Jacob, who derived his descent from Solomon, and Eli, who derived his from Nathan; first how it is that these two, Jacob and Eli, were brothers, and then how it is that their fathers, Matthan and Melchi, although of different families, are declared to be grandfathers of Joseph.

7. Matthan and Melchi having married in succession the same woman, begot children who were uterine brothers, for the law did not prohibit a widow, whether such by divorce or by the death of her husband,

from marrying another.

8. By Estha then (for this was the woman's name according to tradition) Matthan, a descendant of Solomon, first begot Jacob. And when Matthan was dead, Melchi, who traced his descent back to Nathan, being of the same tribe but of another family, married her as before said, and begot a son Eli.

9. Thus we shall find the two, Jacob and Eli, although belonging to different families, yet brethren by the same mother. Of these the one, Jacob, when his brother Eli had died childless, took the latter's wife and begot by her a son Joseph, his own son by nature and in accordance with reason. Wherefore also it is written: 'Jacob begot Joseph.' Matthew 1:6 But according to law he was the son of Eli, for Jacob, being the brother of the latter, raised up seed to him.

10. Hence the genealogy traced through him will not be rendered void, which the evangelist Matthew in his enumeration gives thus: 'Jacob begot Joseph.' But Luke,

on the other hand, says: 'Who was the son, as was supposed' (for this he also adds), 'of Joseph, the son of Eli, the son of Melchi'; for he could not more clearly express the generation according to law. And the expression 'he begot' he has omitted in his genealogical table up to the end, tracing the genealogy back to Adam the son of God. This interpretation is neither incapable of proof nor is it an idle conjecture.

11. For the relatives of our Lord according to the flesh, whether with the desire of boasting or simply wishing to state the fact, in either case truly, have handed down the following account: Some Idumean robbers, having attacked Ascalon, a city of Palestine, carried away from a temple of Apollo which stood near the walls, in addition to other booty, Antipater, son of a certain temple slave named Herod. And since the priest was not able to pay the ransom for his son, Antipater was brought up in the customs of the Idumeans, and afterward was befriended

by Hyrcanus, the high priest of the Jews.

12. And having been sent by Hyrcanus on an embassy to Pompey, and having restored to him the kingdom which had been invaded by his brother Aristobulus, he had the good fortune to be named procurator of Palestine. But Antipater having been slain by those who were envious of his great good fortune was succeeded by his son Herod, who was afterward, by a decree of the senate, made King of the Jews under Antony and Augustus. His sons were Herod and the other tetrarchs. These accounts agree also with those of the Greeks.

13. But as there had been kept in the archives up to that time the genealogies of the Hebrews as well as of those who traced their lineage back to proselytes, such as Achior the Ammonite and Ruth the Moabitess, and to those who were mingled with the Israelites and came out of Egypt with them, Herod, inasmuch as the lineage of the Israelites contributed nothing to

his advantage, and since he was goaded with the consciousness of his own ignoble extraction, burned all the genealogical records, thinking that he might appear of noble origin if no one else were able, from the public registers, to trace back his lineage to the patriarchs or proselytes and to those mingled with them, who were called Georae.

14. A few of the careful, however, having obtained private records of their own, either by remembering the names or by getting them in some other way from the registers, pride themselves on preserving the memory of their noble extraction. Among these are those already mentioned, called Desposyni, on account of their connection with the family of the Saviour. Coming from Nazara and Cochaba, villages of Judea, into other parts of the world, they drew the aforesaid genealogy from memory and from the book of daily records as faithfully as possible.

15. Whether then the case stand thus or

not no one could find a clearer explanation, according to my own opinion and that of every candid person. And let this suffice us, for, although we can urge no testimony in its support, we have nothing better or truer to offer. In any case the Gospel states the truth. And at the end of the same epistle he adds these words: **"Matthan, who was descended from Solomon, begot Jacob. And when Matthan was dead, Melchi, who was descended from Nathan begot Eli by the same woman. Eli and Jacob were thus uterine brothers. Eli having died childless, Jacob raised up seed to him, begetting Joseph, his own son by nature, but by law the son of Eli. Thus Joseph was the son of both."**

17. Thus far Africanus. And the lineage of Joseph being thus traced, Mary also is virtually shown to be of the same tribe with him, since, according to the law of Moses, intermarriages between different tribes were not permitted. For the command is to

marry one of the same family and lineage, so that the inheritance may not pass from tribe to tribe. This may suffice here.

CHAPTER EIGHT

The Cruelty of Herod toward the Infants, and the Manner of his Death

1. WHEN CHRIST WAS BORN, according to the prophecies, in Bethlehem of Judea, at the time indicated, Herod was not a little disturbed by the enquiry of the magi who came from the east, asking where he who was born King of the Jews was to be found –

for they had seen his star, and this was their reason for taking so long a journey; for they earnestly desired to worship the infant as God, – for he imagined that his kingdom might be endangered; and he enquired therefore of the doctors of the law, who belonged to the Jewish nation, where they expected Christ to be born. When he learned that the prophecy of Micah Micah 5:2 announced that Bethlehem was to be his birthplace he commanded, in a single edict, all the male infants in Bethlehem, and all its borders, that were two years of age or less, according to the time which he had accurately ascertained from the magi, to be slain, supposing that Jesus, as was indeed likely, would share the same fate as the others of his own age.

2. But the child anticipated the snare, being carried into Egypt by his parents, who had learned from an angel that appeared unto them what was about to happen. These things are recorded by the Holy Scriptures in the Gospel. Matthew 2

3. It is worth while, in addition to this, to observe the reward which Herod received for his daring crime against Christ and those of the same age. For immediately, without the least delay, the divine vengeance overtook him while he was still alive, and gave him a foretaste of what he was to receive after death.

4. It is not possible to relate here how he tarnished the supposed felicity of his reign by successive calamities in his family, by the murder of wife and children, and others of his nearest relatives and dearest friends. The account, which casts every other tragic drama into the shade, is detailed at length in the histories of Josephus.

5. How, immediately after his crime against our Saviour and the other infants, the punishment sent by God drove him on to his death, we can best learn from the words of that historian who, in the seventeenth book of his Antiquities of the Jews, writes as follows concerning his end:

6. But the disease of Herod grew more severe, God inflicting punishment for his crimes. For a slow fire burned in him which was not so apparent to those who touched him, but augmented his internal distress; for he had a terrible desire for food which it was not possible to resist. He was affected also with ulceration of the intestines, and with especially severe pains in the colon, while a watery and transparent humor settled about his feet.

7. He suffered also from a similar trouble in his abdomen. Nay more, his privy member was putrefied and produced worms. He found also excessive difficulty in breathing, and it was particularly disagreeable because of the offensiveness of the odor and the rapidity of respiration.

8. He had convulsions also in every limb, which gave him uncontrollable strength. It was said, indeed, by those who possessed the power of divination and wisdom to explain such events, that God had inflicted

this punishment upon the King on account of his great impiety.

9. The writer mentioned above recounts these things in the work referred to. And in the second book of his History he gives a similar account of the same Herod, which runs as follows: The disease then seized upon his whole body and distracted it by various torments. For he had a slow fever, and the itching of the skin of his whole body was insupportable. He suffered also from continuous pains in his colon, and there were swellings on his feet like those of a person suffering from dropsy, while his abdomen was inflamed and his privy member so putrefied as to produce worms. Besides this he could breathe only in an upright posture, and then only with difficulty, and he had convulsions in all his limbs, so that the diviners said that his diseases were a punishment.

10. But he, although wrestling with such sufferings, nevertheless clung to life and

hoped for safety, and devised methods of cure. For instance, crossing over Jordan he used the warm baths at Callirhoë, which flow into the Lake Asphaltites, but are themselves sweet enough to drink.

11. His physicians here thought that they could warm his whole body again by means of heated oil. But when they had let him down into a tub filled with oil, his eyes became weak and turned up like the eyes of a dead person. But when his attendants raised an outcry, he recovered at the noise; but finally, despairing of a cure, he commanded about fifty drachms to be distributed among the soldiers, and great sums to be given to his generals and friends.

12. Then returning he came to Jericho, where, being seized with melancholy, he planned to commit an impious deed, as if challenging death itself. For, collecting from every town the most illustrious men of all Judea, he commanded that they be shut up in the so-called hippodrome.

13. And having summoned Salome, his sister, and her husband, Alexander, he said: 'I know that the Jews will rejoice at my death. But I may be lamented by others and have a splendid funeral if you are willing to perform my commands. When I shall expire surround these men, who are now under guard, as quickly as possible with soldiers, and slay them, in order that all Judea and every house may weep for me even against their will.'

14. And after a little Josephus says, **"And again he was so tortured by want of food and by a convulsive cough that, overcome by his pains, he planned to anticipate his fate. Taking an apple he asked also for a knife, for he was accustomed to cut apples and eat them. Then looking round to see that there was no one to hinder, he raised his right hand as if to stab himself."**

15. In addition to these things the same writer records that he slew another of his

own sons before his death, the third one slain by his command, and that immediately afterward he breathed his last, not without excessive pain.

16. Such was the end of Herod, who suffered a just punishment for his slaughter of the children of Bethlehem, which was the result of his plots against our Saviour.

17. After this an angel appeared in a dream to Joseph in Egypt and commanded him to go to Judea with the child and its mother, revealing to him that those who had sought the life of the child were dead. To this the evangelist adds, **"But when he heard that Archelaus did reign in the room of his father Herod he was afraid to go there; notwithstanding being warned of God in a dream he turned aside into the parts of Galilee."** Matthew 2:22

CHAPTER NINE

The Times of Pilate

1. THE HISTORIAN ALREADY mentioned agrees with the evangelist in regard to the fact that Archelaus succeeded to the government after Herod. He records the manner in which he received the kingdom of the Jews by the will of his father Herod and by the decree of Cæsar Augustus, and how, after he had reigned ten years, he lost his kingdom, and his brothers Philip

and Herod the younger, with Lysanias, still ruled their own tetrarchies. The same writer, in the eighteenth book of his Antiquities, says that about the twelfth year of the reign of Tiberius, who had succeeded to the empire after Augustus had ruled fifty-seven years, Pontius Pilate was entrusted with the government of Judea, and that he remained there ten full years, almost until the death of Tiberius.

2. Accordingly the forgery of those who have recently given currency to acts against our Saviour is clearly proved. For the very date given in them shows the falsehood of their fabricators.

3. For the things which they have dared to say concerning the passion of the Saviour are put into the fourth consulship of Tiberius, which occurred in the seventh year of his reign; at which time it is plain that Pilate was not yet ruling in Judea, if the testimony of Josephus is to be believed, who clearly shows in the above-mentioned

work that Pilate was made procurator of Judea by Tiberius in the twelfth year of his reign.

CHAPTER TEN

The High Priests of the Jews under whom Christ taught

1. IT WAS IN THE fifteenth year of the reign of Tiberius, according to the evangelist, and in the fourth year of the governorship of Pontius Pilate, while Herod and Lysanias and Philip were ruling the rest of Judea, that our Saviour and Lord, Jesus the Christ of God, being about thirty years of age, came to John for baptism and began the

promulgation of the Gospel.

2. The Divine Scripture says, moreover, that he passed the entire time of his ministry under the high priests Annas and Caiaphas, showing that in the time which belonged to the priesthood of those two men the whole period of his teaching was completed. Since he began his work during the high priesthood of Annas and taught until Caiaphas held the office, the entire time does not comprise quite four years.

3. For the rites of the law having been already abolished since that time, the customary usages in connection with the worship of God, according to which the high priest acquired his office by hereditary descent and held it for life, were also annulled and there were appointed to the high priesthood by the Roman governors now one and now another person who continued in office not more than one year.

4. Josephus relates that there were four high priests in succession from Annas to

Caiaphas. Thus in the same book of the Antiquities he writes as follows: **"Valerius Gratus having put an end to the priesthood of Ananus appoints Ishmael, the son of Fabi, high priest. And having removed him after a little he appoints Eleazer, the son of Ananus the high priest, to the same office. And having removed him also at the end of a year he gives the high priesthood to Simon, the son of Camithus. But he likewise held the honor no more than a year, when Josephus, called also Caiaphas, succeeded him."** Accordingly the whole time of our Saviour's ministry is shown to have been not quite four full years, four high priests, from Annas to the accession of Caiaphas, having held office a year each. The Gospel therefore has rightly indicated Caiaphas as the high priest under whom the Saviour suffered. From which also we can see that the time of our Saviour's ministry does not disagree with the foregoing investigation.

5. Our Saviour and Lord, not long after the beginning of his ministry, called the twelve apostles, and these alone of all his disciples he named apostles, as a special honor. And again he appointed seventy others whom he sent out two by two before his face into every place and city whither he himself was about to come.

CHAPTER ELEVEN

Testimonies in Regard to John the Baptist and Christ

1. NOT LONG AFTER THIS John the Baptist was beheaded by the younger Herod, as is stated in the Gospels. Josephus also records the same fact, making mention of Herodias by name, and stating that, although she was the wife of his brother, Herod made her his own wife after divorcing his former lawful wife, who

was the daughter of Aretas, king of Petra, and separating Herodias from her husband while he was still alive.

2. It was on her account also that he slew John, and waged war with Aretas, because of the disgrace inflicted on the daughter of the latter. Josephus relates that in this war, when they came to battle, Herod's entire army was destroyed, and that he suffered this calamity on account of his crime against John.

3. The same Josephus confesses in this account that John the Baptist was an exceedingly righteous man, and thus agrees with the things written of him in the Gospels. He records also that Herod lost his kingdom on account of the same Herodias, and that he was driven into banishment with her, and condemned to live at Vienne in Gaul.

4. He relates these things in the eighteenth book of the Antiquities, where he writes of John in the following words: It seemed to some of the Jews that the army of Herod

was destroyed by God, who most justly avenged John called the Baptist.

5. For Herod slew him, a good man and one who exhorted the Jews to come and receive baptism, practicing virtue and exercising righteousness toward each other and toward God; for baptism would appear acceptable unto Him when they employed it, not for the remission of certain sins, but for the purification of the body, as the soul had been already purified in righteousness.

6. And when others gathered about him (for they found much pleasure in listening to his words), Herod feared that his great influence might lead to some sedition, for they appeared ready to do whatever he might advise. He therefore considered it much better, before any new thing should be done under John's influence, to anticipate it by slaying him, than to repent after revolution had come, and when he found himself in the midst of difficulties. On account of Herod's suspicion John

was sent in bonds to the above-mentioned citadel of Machæra, and there slain.

7. After relating these things concerning John, he makes mention of our Saviour in the same work, in the following words: And there lived at that time Jesus, a wise man, if indeed it be proper to call him a man. For he was a doer of wonderful works, and a teacher of such men as receive the truth in gladness. And he attached to himself many of the Jews, and many also of the Greeks. He was the Christ.

8. When Pilate, on the accusation of our principal men, condemned him to the cross, those who had loved him in the beginning did not cease loving him. For he appeared unto them again alive on the third day, the divine prophets having told these and countless other wonderful things concerning him. Moreover, the race of Christians, named after him, continues down to the present day.

9. Since an historian, who is one of the

Hebrews themselves, has recorded in his work these things concerning John the Baptist and our Saviour, what excuse is there left for not convicting them of being destitute of all shame, who have forged the acts against them? But let this suffice here.

CHAPTER TWELVE

The Disciples of our Saviour

1. THE NAMES OF THE apostles of our Saviour are known to every one from the Gospels. But there exists no catalogue of the seventy disciples. Barnabas, indeed, is said to have been one of them, of whom the Acts of the Apostles makes mention in various places, and especially Paul in his Epistle to the Galatians.

2. They say that Sosthenes also, who wrote to the Corinthians with Paul, was one

of them. This is the account of Clement in the fifth book of his Hypotyposes, in which he also says that Cephas was one of the seventy disciples, a man who bore the same name as the apostle Peter, and the one concerning whom Paul says, **"When Cephas came to Antioch I withstood him to his face."** Galatians 2:11

3. Matthias, also, who was numbered with the apostles in the place of Judas, and the one who was honored by being made a candidate with him, are likewise said to have been deemed worthy of the same calling with the seventy. They say that Thaddeus also was one of them, concerning whom I shall presently relate an account which has come down to us. And upon examination you will find that our Saviour had more than seventy disciples, according to the testimony of Paul, who says that after his resurrection from the dead he appeared first to Cephas, then to the twelve, and after them to above five hundred brethren at once, of whom some had fallen

asleep; 1 Corinthians 15:5-7 but the majority were still living at the time he wrote.

4. Afterwards he says he appeared unto James, who was one of the so-called brethren of the Saviour. But, since in addition to these, there were many others who were called apostles, in imitation of the Twelve, as was Paul himself, he adds: **"Afterward he appeared to all the apostles."** 1 Corinthians 15:7 So much in regard to these persons. But the story concerning Thaddeus is as follows.

CHAPTER THIRTEEN

Narrative concerning the Prince of the Edessenes

1. THE DIVINITY OF OUR Lord and Saviour Jesus Christ being reported abroad among all men on account of his wonder-working power, he attracted countless numbers from foreign countries lying far away from Judea, who had the hope of being cured of their diseases and of all kinds of sufferings.

2. For instance the King Abgarus, who

ruled with great glory the nations beyond the Euphrates, being afflicted with a terrible disease which it was beyond the power of human skill to cure, when he heard of the name of Jesus, and of his miracles, which were attested by all with one accord sent a message to him by a courier and begged him to heal his disease.

3. But he did not at that time comply with his request; yet he deemed him worthy of a personal letter in which he said that he would send one of his disciples to cure his disease, and at the same time promised salvation to himself and all his house.

4. Not long afterward his promise was fulfilled. For after his resurrection from the dead and his ascent into heaven, Thomas, one of the twelve apostles, under divine impulse sent Thaddeus, who was also numbered among the seventy disciples of Christ, to Edessa, as a preacher and evangelist of the teaching of Christ.

5. And all that our Saviour had promised

received through him its fulfillment. You have written evidence of these things taken from the archives of Edessa, which was at that time a royal city. For in the public registers there, which contain accounts of ancient times and the acts of Abgarus, these things have been found preserved down to the present time. But there is no better way than to hear the epistles themselves which we have taken from the archives and have literally translated from the Syriac language in the following manner.

Copy of an epistle written by Abgarus the ruler to Jesus, and sent to him at Jerusalem by Ananias the swift courier.

6. Abgarus, ruler of Edessa, to Jesus the excellent Saviour who has appeared in the country of Jerusalem, greeting. I have heard the reports of you and of your cures as performed by you without medicines or herbs. For it is said that you make the blind to see and the lame to walk, that you cleanse lepers and cast out impure spirits and demons, and

that you heal those afflicted with lingering disease, and raise the dead.

7. And having heard all these things concerning you, I have concluded that one of two things must be true: either you are God, and having come down from heaven you do these things, or else you, who does these things, are the Son of God.

8. I have therefore written to you to ask you if you would take the trouble to come to me and heal the disease which I have. For I have heard that the Jews are murmuring against you and are plotting to injure you. But I have a very small yet noble city which is great enough for us both.

The answer of Jesus to the ruler Abgarus by the courier Ananias.

9. **"Blessed are you who hast believed in me without having seen me. For it is written concerning me, that they who have seen me will not believe in me, and that they who have not seen me will believe and be saved. But in regard to**

what you have written me, that I should come to you, it is necessary for me to fulfill all things here for which I have been sent, and after I have fulfilled them thus to be taken up again to him that sent me. But after I have been taken up I will send to you one of my disciples, that he may heal your disease and give life to you and yours."

Further accounts

10. To these epistles there was added the following account in the Syriac language. After the ascension of Jesus, Judas, who was also called Thomas, sent to him Thaddeus, an apostle, one of the Seventy. When he had come he lodged with Tobias, the son of Tobias. When the report of him got abroad, it was told Abgarus that an apostle of Jesus had come, as he had written him.

11. Thaddeus began then in the power of God to heal every disease and infirmity, insomuch that all wondered. And when Abgarus heard of the great and wonderful

things which he did and of the cures which he performed, he began to suspect that he was the one of whom Jesus had written him, saying, 'After I have been taken up I will send to you one of my disciples who will heal you.'

12. Therefore, summoning Tobias, with whom Thaddeus lodged, he said, I have heard that a certain man of power has come and is lodging in your house. Bring him to me. And Tobias coming to Thaddeus said to him, The ruler Abgarus summoned me and told me to bring you to him that you might heal him. And Thaddeus said, I will go, for I have been sent to him with power.

13. Tobias therefore arose early on the following day, and taking Thaddeus came to Abgarus. And when he came, the nobles were present and stood about Abgarus. And immediately upon his entrance a great vision appeared to Abgarus in the countenance of the apostle Thaddeus. When Abgarus saw it he prostrated himself before Thaddeus,

while all those who stood about were astonished; for they did not see the vision, which appeared to Abgarus alone.

14. He then asked Thaddeus if he were in truth a disciple of Jesus the Son of God, who had said to him, 'I will send you one of my disciples, who shall heal you and give you life.' And Thaddeus said, Because you have mightily believed in him that sent me, therefore have I been sent unto you. And still further, if you believe in him, the petitions of your heart shall be granted you as you believe.

15. And Abgarus said to him, So much have I believed in him that I wished to take an army and destroy those Jews who crucified him, had I not been deterred from it by reason of the dominion of the Romans. And Thaddeus said, Our Lord has fulfilled the will of his Father, and having fulfilled it has been taken up to his Father. And Abgarus said to him, I too have believed in him and in his Father.

16. And Thaddeus said to him, Therefore

I place my hand upon you in his name. And when he had done it, immediately Abgarus was cured of the disease and of the suffering which he had.

17. And Abgarus marvelled, that as he had heard concerning Jesus, so he had received in very deed through his disciple Thaddeus, who healed him without medicines and herbs, and not only him, but also Abdus the son of Abdus, who was afflicted with the gout; for he too came to him and fell at his feet, and having received a benediction by the imposition of his hands, he was healed. The same Thaddeus cured also many other inhabitants of the city, and did wonders and marvelous works, and preached the word of God.

18. And afterward Abgarus said, You, O Thaddeus, do these things with the power of God, and we marvel. But, in addition to these things, I pray you to inform me in regard to the coming of Jesus, how he was born; and in regard to his power, by what

power he performed those deeds of which I have heard.

19. And Thaddeus said, Now indeed will I keep silence, since I have been sent to proclaim the word publicly. But tomorrow assemble for me all your citizens, and I will preach in their presence and sow among them the word of God, concerning the coming of Jesus, how he was born; and concerning his mission, for what purpose he was sent by the Father; and concerning the power of his works, and the mysteries which he proclaimed in the world, and by what power he did these things; and concerning his new preaching, and his abasement and humiliation, and how he humbled himself, and died and debased his divinity and was crucified, and descended into Hades, and burst the bars which from eternity had not been broken, and raised the dead; for he descended alone, but rose with many, and thus ascended to his Father.

20. Abgarus therefore commanded the

citizens to assemble early in the morning to hear the preaching of Thaddeus, and afterward he ordered gold and silver to be given him. But he refused to take it, saying, If we have forsaken that which was our own, how shall we take that which is another's? These things were done in the three hundred and fortieth year.

I have inserted them here in their proper place, translated from the Syriac literally, and I hope to good purpose.

BOOK TWO

Introduction

1. WE HAVE DISCUSSED IN the preceding book those subjects in ecclesiastical history which it was necessary to treat by way of introduction, and have accompanied them with brief proofs. Such were the divinity of the saving Word, and the antiquity of the doctrines which we teach, as well as of that

evangelical life which is led by Christians, together with the events which have taken place in connection with Christ's recent appearance, and in connection with his passion and with the choice of the apostles.

2. In the present book let us examine the events which took place after his ascension, confirming some of them from the divine Scriptures, and others from such writings as we shall refer to from time to time.

CHAPTER ONE

The Course pursued by the Apostles after the Ascension of Christ

1. FIRST, THEN, IN THE place of Judas, the betrayer, Matthias, who, as has been shown was also one of the Seventy, was chosen to the apostolate. And there were appointed to the diaconate, for the service of the congregation, by prayer and the

laying on of the hands of the apostles, approved men, seven in number, of whom Stephen was one. He first, after the Lord, was stoned to death at the time of his ordination by the slayers of the Lord, as if he had been promoted for this very purpose. And thus he was the first to receive the crown, corresponding to his name, which belongs to the martyrs of Christ, who are worthy of the meed of victory.

2. Then James, whom the ancients surnamed the Just on account of the excellence of his virtue, is recorded to have been the first to be made bishop of the church of Jerusalem. This James was called the brother of the Lord because he was known as a son of Joseph, and Joseph was supposed to be the father of Christ, because the Virgin, being betrothed to him, **"was found with child by the Holy Ghost before they came together,"** Matthew 1:18 as the account of the holy Gospels shows.

3. But Clement in the sixth book of his

Hypotyposes writes thus: **"For they say that Peter and James and John after the ascension of our Saviour, as if also preferred by our Lord, strove not after honor, but chose James the Just bishop of Jerusalem."**

4. But the same writer, in the seventh book of the same work, relates also the following things concerning him: **"The Lord after his resurrection imparted knowledge to James the Just and to John and Peter, and they imparted it to the rest of the apostles, and the rest of the apostles to the seventy, of whom Barnabas was one. But there were two Jameses: one called the Just, who was thrown from the pinnacle of the temple and was beaten to death with a club by a fuller, and another who was beheaded."** Paul also makes mention of the same James the Just, where he writes, **"Other of the apostles saw I none, save James the Lord's brother."** Galatians 1:19

5. At that time also the promise of our Saviour to the king of the Osrhœnians was fulfilled. For Thomas, under a divine impulse, sent Thaddeus to Edessa as a preacher and evangelist of the religion of Christ, as we have shown a little above from the document found there.

7. When he came to that place he healed Abgarus by the word of Christ; and after bringing all the people there into the right attitude of mind by means of his works, and leading them to adore the power of Christ, he made them disciples of the Saviour's teaching. And from that time down to the present the whole city of the Edessenes has been devoted to the name of Christ, offering no common proof of the beneficence of our Saviour toward them also.

8. These things have been drawn from ancient accounts; but let us now turn again to the divine Scripture. When the first and greatest persecution was instigated by the Jews against the church of Jerusalem in

connection with the martyrdom of Stephen, and when all the disciples, except the Twelve, were scattered throughout Judea and Samaria, some, as the divine Scripture says, went as far as Phœnicia and Cyprus and Antioch, but could not yet venture to impart the word of faith to the nations, and therefore preached it to the Jews alone.

9. During this time Paul was still persecuting the church, and entering the houses of believers was dragging men and women away and committing them to prison.

10. Philip also, one of those who with Stephen had been entrusted with the diaconate, being among those who were scattered abroad, went down to Samaria, and being filled with the divine power, he first preached the word to the inhabitants of that country. And divine grace worked so mightily with him that even Simon Magus with many others was attracted by his words.

11. Simon was at that time so celebrated, and had acquired, by his juggglery, such

influence over those who were deceived by him, that he was thought to be the Great Power of God. [According to Eusebius here, Simon Magus was called τὴν μεγ€λην δύναμιν τοῦ θεοῦ. In Acts 8:10, he was called ἡ δύναμις τοῦ θεοῦ ἡ καλουμένη. According to Irenæus (I.23.1) he was called "the loftiest of all powers, that is, the one who is father over all things" (sublissimam virtutem, hoc est, eum qui sit nuper omnia Pater). According to Justin Martyr (Apology I.26), he was called τὸν πρῶτον θεόν. According to the Clementine Homilies (II.22) he wished to be called "a certain supreme power of God" (ἁ νωτ€τη τις δύναμις). According to the Clementine Recognitions (II.7) he was called the "Standing One" (hinc ergo Stans appellatur).]

But at this time, being amazed at the wonderful deeds wrought by Philip through the divine power, he feigned and counterfeited faith in Christ, even going so far as to receive baptism.

12. And what is surprising, the same thing is done even to this day by those who follow his most impure heresy. For they, after the manner of their forefather, slipping into the Church, like a pestilential and leprous disease greatly afflict those into whom they are able to infuse the deadly and terrible poison concealed in themselves. The most of these have been expelled as soon as they have been caught in their wickedness, as Simon himself, when detected by Peter, received the merited punishment.

13. But as the preaching of the Saviour's Gospel was daily advancing, a certain providence led from the land of the Ethiopians an officer of the queen of that country, for Ethiopia even to the present day is ruled, according to ancestral custom, by a woman. He, first among the Gentiles, received of the mysteries of the divine word from Philip in consequence of a revelation, and having become the first-fruits of believers throughout the world, he is said to have been the first

on returning to his country to proclaim the knowledge of the God of the universe and the life-giving sojourn of our Saviour among men; so that through him in truth the prophecy obtained its fulfillment, which declares that **"Ethiopia stretches out her hand unto God."**

14. In addition to these, Paul, that **"chosen vessel,"** Acts 9:15 **"not of men neither through men, but by the revelation of Jesus Christ himself and of God the Father who raised him from the dead,"** Galatians 1:1 was appointed an apostle, being made worthy of the call by a vision and by a voice which was uttered in a revelation from heaven.

CHAPTER TWO

How Tiberius was affected when informed by Pilate Concerning Christ

1. AND WHEN THE WONDERFUL resurrection and ascension of our Saviour were already reported abroad, in accordance with an ancient custom which prevailed among the rulers of the provinces, of reporting to the emperor the

novel occurrences which took place in them, in order that nothing might escape him, Pontius Pilate informed Tiberius of the reports which were reported abroad through all Palestine concerning the resurrection of our Saviour Jesus from the dead.

2. He gave an account also of other wonders which he had learned of him, and how, after his death, having risen from the dead, he was now believed by many to be a God. They say that Tiberius referred the matter to the Senate, but that they rejected it, ostensibly because they had not first examined into the matter (for an ancient law prevailed that no one should be made a God by the Romans except by a vote and decree of the Senate), but in reality because the saving teaching of the divine Gospel did not need the confirmation and recommendation of men.

3. But although the Senate of the Romans rejected the proposition made in regard to our Saviour, Tiberius still retained the opinion

which he had held at first, and contrived no hostile measures against Christ.

4. These things are recorded by Tertullian, a man well versed in the laws of the Romans, and in other respects of high repute, and one of those especially distinguished in Rome. In his apology for the Christians, which was written by him in the Latin language, and has been translated into Greek, he writes as follows:

5. But in order that we may give an account of these laws from their origin, it was an ancient decree that no one should be consecrated a God by the emperor until the Senate had expressed its approval. Marcus Aurelius did thus concerning a certain idol, Alburnus. And this is a point in favor of our doctrine, that among you divine dignity is conferred by human decree. If a God does not please a man he is not made a God. Thus, according to this custom, it is necessary for man to be gracious to God.

6. Tiberius, therefore, under whom the

name of Christ made its entry into the world, when this doctrine was reported to him from Palestine, where it first began, communicated with the Senate, making it clear to them that he was pleased with the doctrine. But the Senate, since it had not itself proved the matter, rejected it. But Tiberius continued to hold his own opinion, and threatened death to the accusers of the Christians. Heavenly providence had wisely instilled this into his mind in order that the doctrine of the Gospel, unhindered at its beginning, might spread in all directions throughout the world.

CHAPTER THREE

The Doctrine of Christ
soon spread throughout
All the World

1. THUS, UNDER THE INFLUENCE of heavenly power, and with the divine co-operation, the doctrine of the Saviour, like the rays of the sun, quickly illumined the whole world; and straightway, in accordance with the divine Scriptures, the voice of the

inspired evangelists and apostles went forth through all the earth, and their words to the end of the world.

2. In every city and village, churches were quickly established, filled with multitudes of people like a replenished threshing-floor. And those whose minds, in consequence of errors which had descended to them from their forefathers, were fettered by the ancient disease of idolatrous superstition, were, by the power of Christ operating through the teaching and the wonderful works of his disciples, set free, as it were, from terrible masters, and found a release from the most cruel bondage. They renounced with abhorrence every species of demoniacal polytheism, and confessed that there was only one God, the creator of all things, and him they honored with the rites of true piety, through the inspired and rational worship which has been planted by our Saviour among men.

3. But the divine grace being now poured

out upon the rest of the nations, Cornelius, of Cæsarea in Palestine, with his whole house, through a divine revelation and the agency of Peter, first received faith in Christ; and after him a multitude of other Greeks in Antioch, to whom those who were scattered by the persecution of Stephen had preached the Gospel. When the church of Antioch was now increasing and abounding, and a multitude of prophets from Jerusalem were on the ground, among them Barnabas and Paul and in addition many other brethren, the name of Christians first sprang up there, as from a fresh and life-giving fountain.

4. And Agabus, one of the prophets who was with them, uttered a prophecy concerning the famine which was about to take place, and Paul and Barnabas were sent to relieve the necessities of the brethren.

After the Death of Tiberius, Caius appointed Agrippa King of the Jews, having punished Herod with Perpetual Exile

1. TIBERIUS DIED, after having reigned about twenty-two years, and Caius succeeded him in the empire. He immediately gave the government of the Jews to Agrippa, making him king over the tetrarchies of Philip and of

Lysanias; in addition to which he bestowed upon him, not long afterward, the tetrarchy of Herod, having punished Herod (the one under whom the Saviour suffered) and his wife Herodias with perpetual exile on account of numerous crimes. Josephus is a witness to these facts.

2. Under this emperor, Philo became known; a man most celebrated not only among many of our own, but also among many scholars without the Church. He was a Hebrew by birth, but was inferior to none of those who held high dignities in Alexandria. How exceedingly he labored in the Scriptures and in the studies of his nation is plain to all from the work which he has done. How familiar he was with philosophy and with the liberal studies of foreign nations, it is not necessary to say, since he is reported to have surpassed all his contemporaries in the study of Platonic and Pythagorean philosophy, to which he particularly devoted his attention.

CHAPTER FIVE

Philo's Embassy to Caius in Behalf of the Jews

1. PHILO HAS GIVEN US an account, in five books, of the misfortunes of the Jews under Caius. He recounts at the same time the madness of Caius: how he called himself a god, and performed as emperor innumerable acts of tyranny; and he describes further the miseries of the Jews under him, and gives a report of the embassy upon which

he himself was sent to Rome in behalf of his fellow-countrymen in Alexandria; how when he appeared before Caius in behalf of the laws of his fathers he received nothing but laughter and ridicule, and almost incurred the risk of his life.

2. Josephus also makes mention of these things in the eighteenth book of his Antiquities, in the following words: A sedition having arisen in Alexandria between the Jews that dwell there and the Greeks, three deputies were chosen from each faction and went to Caius.

3. One of the Alexandrian deputies was Apion, who uttered many slanders against the Jews; among other things saying that they neglected the honors due to Cæsar. For while all other subjects of Rome erected altars and temples to Caius, and in all other respects treated him just as they did the gods, they alone considered it disgraceful to honor him with statues and to swear by his name.

4. And when Apion had uttered many severe charges by which he hoped that Caius would be aroused, as indeed was likely, Philo, the chief of the Jewish embassy, a man celebrated in every respect, a brother of Alexander the Alabarch, and not unskilled in philosophy, was prepared to enter upon a defense in reply to his accusations.

5. But Caius prevented him and ordered him to leave, and being very angry, it was plain that he meditated some severe measure against them. And Philo departed covered with insult and told the Jews that were with him to be of good courage; for while Caius was raging against them he was in fact already contending with God.

6. Thus far Josephus. And Philo himself, in the work **On the Embassy** which he wrote, describes accurately and in detail the things which were done by him at that time. But I shall omit the most of them and record only those things which will make clearly evident to the reader that the misfortunes of the Jews

came upon them not long after their daring deeds against Christ and on account of the same.

7. And in the first place he relates that at Rome in the reign of Tiberius, Sejanus, who at that time enjoyed great influence with the emperor, made every effort to destroy the Jewish nation utterly; and that in Judea, Pilate, under whom the crimes against the Saviour were committed, attempted something contrary to the Jewish law in respect to the temple, which was at that time still standing in Jerusalem, and excited them to the greatest tumults.

The Misfortunes which overwhelmed the Jews after their Presumption against Christ

1. AFTER THE DEATH OF Tiberius, Caius received the empire, and, besides innumerable other acts of tyranny against many people, he greatly afflicted especially the whole nation of the Jews. These things

we may learn briefly from the words of Philo, who writes as follows:

2. **"So great was the caprice of Caius in his conduct toward all, and especially toward the nation of the Jews. The latter he so bitterly hated that he appropriated to himself their places of worship in the other cities, and beginning with Alexandria he filled them with images and statues of himself (for in permitting others to erect them he really erected them himself). The temple in the holy city, which had hitherto been left untouched, and had been regarded as an inviolable asylum, he altered and transformed into a temple of his own, that it might be called the temple of the visible Jupiter, the younger Caius."**

3. Innumerable other terrible and almost indescribable calamities which came upon the Jews in Alexandria during the reign of the same emperor, are recorded by the same author in a second work, to which he gave

the title, **On the Virtues**. With him agrees also Josephus, who likewise indicates that the misfortunes of the whole nation began with the time of Pilate, and with their daring crimes against the Saviour.

4. Hear what he says in the second book of his Jewish War, where he writes as follows: **"Pilate being sent to Judea as procurator by Tiberius, secretly carried veiled images of the emperor, called ensigns, to Jerusalem by night. The following day this caused the greatest disturbance among the Jews. For those who were near were confounded at the sight, beholding their laws, as it were, trampled under foot. For they allow no image to be set up in their city."**

5. Comparing these things with the writings of the evangelists, you will see that it was not long before there came upon them the penalty for the exclamation which they had uttered under the same Pilate, when they cried out that they had no other king than

Cæsar. John 19:15

6. The same writer further records that after this another calamity overtook them. He writes as follows: After this he stirred up another tumult by making use of the holy treasure, which is called Corban, in the construction of an aqueduct three hundred stadia in length.

7. The multitude were greatly displeased at it, and when Pilate was in Jerusalem they surrounded his tribunal and gave utterance to loud complaints. But he, anticipating the tumult, had distributed through the crowd armed soldiers disguised in citizen's clothing, forbidding them to use the sword, but commanding them to strike with clubs those who should make an outcry. To them he now gave the preconcerted signal from the tribunal. And the Jews being beaten, many of them perished in consequence of the blows, while many others were trampled under foot by their own countrymen in their flight, and thus lost their lives. But the

multitude, overawed by the fate of those who were slain, held their peace.

8. In addition to these the same author records many other tumults which were stirred up in Jerusalem itself, and shows that from that time seditions and wars and mischievous plots followed each other in quick succession, and never ceased in the city and in all Judea until finally the siege of Vespasian overwhelmed them. Thus the divine vengeance overtook the Jews for the crimes which they dared to commit against Christ.

CHAPTER SEVEN

Pilate's Suicide

IT IS WORTHY OF note that Pilate himself, who was governor in the time of our Saviour, is reported to have fallen into such misfortunes under Caius, whose times we are recording, that he was forced to become his own murderer and executioner; and thus divine vengeance, as it seems, was not long in overtaking him. This is stated by those Greek historians who have recorded the Olympiads, together with the respective events which have taken place in each period.

CHAPTER EIGHT

The Famine which took Place in the Reign of Claudius

1. CAIUS HAD HELD THE power not quite four years, when he was succeeded by the emperor Claudius. Under him the world was visited with a famine, which writers that are entire strangers to our religion have recorded in their histories. And thus the prediction of Agabus recorded in the Acts of the Apostles, Acts 11:28 according to which the whole

world was to be visited by a famine, received its fulfillment.

2. And Luke, in the Acts, after mentioning the famine in the time of Claudius, and stating that the brethren of Antioch, each according to his ability, sent to the brethren of Judea by the hands of Paul and Barnabas, Acts 11:29-30 adds the following account.

CHAPTER NINE

The Martyrdom of James the Apostle

1. " **ACTS 12:1-2 NOW ABOUT** that **time**" (it is clear that he means the time of Claudius) **"Herod the King stretched forth his hands to vex certain of the Church. And he killed James the brother of John with the sword."**

2. And concerning this James, Clement, in the seventh book of his Hypotyposes, relates

a story which is worthy of mention; telling it as he received it from those who had lived before him. He says that the one who led James to the judgment-seat, when he saw him bearing his testimony, was moved, and confessed that he was himself also a Christian.

3. They were both therefore, he says, led away together; and on the way he begged James to forgive him. And he, after considering a little, said, **"Peace be with you,"** and kissed him. And thus they were both beheaded at the same time.

4. And then, as the divine Scripture says, Acts 12:3 sqq. Herod, upon the death of James, seeing that the deed pleased the Jews, attacked Peter also and committed him to prison, and would have slain him if he had not, by the divine appearance of an angel who came to him by night, been wonderfully released from his bonds, and thus liberated for the service of the Gospel. Such was the providence of God in respect to Peter.

CHAPTER TEN

Agrippa, who was also called Herod, having persecuted the Apostles, immediately experienced the Divine Vengeance

1. THE CONSEQUENCES OF THE king's undertaking against the apostles were not long deferred, but the avenging minister of divine justice overtook him immediately

159

after his plots against them, as the Book of Acts records. For when he had journeyed to Cæsarea, on a notable feast-day, clothed in a splendid and royal garment, he delivered an address to the people from a lofty throne in front of the tribunal. And when all the multitude applauded the speech, as if it were the voice of a god and not of a man, the Scripture relates that an angel of the Lord smote him, and being eaten of worms he gave up the ghost. Acts 12:23

2. We must admire the account of Josephus for its agreement with the divine Scriptures in regard to this wonderful event; for he clearly bears witness to the truth in the nineteenth book of his Antiquities, where he relates the wonder in the following words:

3. He had completed the third year of his reign over all Judea when he came to Cæsarea, which was formerly called Strato's Tower. northwest of Jerusalem. In the time of Strabo there was simply a small town at this point, called "Strato's Tower"; but about

10 BC Herod the Great built the city of Cæsarea, which soon became the principal Roman city of Palestine, and was noted for its magnificence. It became, later, the seat of an important Christian school, and played quite a part in Church history. Eusebius himself was Bishop of Cæsarea. It was a city of importance, even in the time of the crusades, but is now a scene of utter desolation.}--> There he held games in honor of Cæsar, learning that this was a festival observed in behalf of Cæsar's safety. At this festival was collected a great multitude of the highest and most honorable men in the province.

4. And on the second day of the games he proceeded to the theater at break of day, wearing a garment entirely of silver and of wonderful texture. And there the silver, illuminated by the reflection of the sun's earliest rays, shone marvelously, gleaming so brightly as to produce a sort of fear and terror in those who gazed upon him.

5. And immediately his flatterers, some

from one place, others from another, raised up their voices in a way that was not for his good, calling him a god, and saying, 'Be merciful; if up to this time we have feared you as a man, henceforth we confess that you are superior to the nature of mortals.'

6. The king did not rebuke them, nor did he reject their impious flattery. But after a little, looking up, he saw an angel sitting above his head. And this he quickly perceived would be the cause of evil as it had once been the cause of good fortune, and he was smitten with a heart-piercing pain.

7. And straightway distress, beginning with the greatest violence, seized his bowels. And looking upon his friends he said, 'I, your god, am now commanded to depart this life; and fate thus on the spot disproves the lying words you have just uttered concerning me. He who has been called immortal by you is now led away to die; but our destiny must be accepted as

God has determined it. For we have passed our life by no means ingloriously, but in that splendor which is called happiness.'

8. And when he had said this he labored with an increase of pain. He was accordingly carried in haste to the palace, while the report spread among all that the king would undoubtedly soon die. But the multitude, with their wives and children, sitting on sackcloth after the custom of their fathers, implored God in behalf of the king, and every place was filled with lamentation and tears. And the king as he lay in a lofty chamber, and saw them below lying prostrate on the ground, could not refrain from weeping himself.

9. And after suffering continually for five days with pain in the bowels, he departed this life, in the fifty-fourth year of his age, and in the seventh year of his reign. Four years he ruled under the Emperor Caius – three of them over the tetrarchy of Philip, to which was added in the fourth year that of Herod – and three years during the reign of

the Emperor Claudius.

10. I marvel greatly that Josephus, in these things as well as in others, so fully agrees with the divine Scriptures. But if there should seem to any one to be a disagreement in respect to the name of the king, the time at least and the events show that the same person is meant, whether the change of name has been caused by the error of a copyist, or is due to the fact that he, like so many, bore two names.

CHAPTER ELEVEN

The Martyrdom of James the Apostle

1. LUKE, IN THE ACTS, introduces Gamaliel as saying, at the consultation which was held concerning the apostles, that at the time referred to, **"rose up Theudas boasting himself to be somebody; who was slain; and all, as many as obeyed him, were scattered."** Acts 5:36 Let us therefore add the account of Josephus concerning this

man. He records in the work mentioned just above, the following circumstances:

2. While Fadus was procurator of Judea a certain impostor called Theudas persuaded a very great multitude to take their possessions and follow him to the river Jordan. For he said that he was a prophet, and that the river should be divided at his command, and afford them an easy passage.

3. And with these words he deceived many. But Fadus did not permit them to enjoy their folly, but sent a troop of horsemen against them, who fell upon them unexpectedly and slew many of them and took many others alive, while they took Theudas himself captive, and cut off his head and carried it to Jerusalem. Besides this he also makes mention of the famine, which took place in the reign of Claudius, in the following words.

CHAPTER TWELVE

Helen, the Queen of the Osrhœnians

1. "AND AT THIS TIME it came to pass that the great famine took place in Judea, in which the queen Helen, having purchased grain from Egypt with large sums, distributed it to the needy."

2. You will find this statement also in agreement with the Acts of the Apostles, where it is said that the disciples at

Antioch, **"each according to his ability, determined to send relief to the brethren that dwelt in Judea; which also they did, and sent it to the elders by the hands of Barnabas and Paul."**

3. But splendid monuments of this Helen, of whom the historian has made mention, are still shown in the suburbs of the city which is now caled Ælia. But she is said to have been queen of the Adiabeni.

CHAPTER THIRTEEN

Simon Magus

1. BUT FAITH IN OUR Saviour and Lord Jesus Christ having now been diffused among all men, the enemy of man's salvation contrived a plan for seizing the imperial city for himself. He conducted there the above-mentioned Simon, aided him in his deceitful arts, led many of the inhabitants of Rome astray, and thus brought them into his own power.

2. This is stated by Justin, one of our

distinguished writers who lived not long after the time of the apostles. Concerning him I shall speak in the proper place. Take and read the work of this man, who in the first Apology which he addressed to Antonine in behalf of our religion writes as follows:

3. And after the ascension of the Lord into heaven the demons put forward certain men who said they were gods, and who were not only allowed by you to go unpersecuted, but were even deemed worthy of honors. One of them was Simon, a Samaritan of the village of Gitto, who in the reign of Claudius Cæsar performed in your imperial city some mighty acts of magic by the art of demons operating in him, and was considered a god, and as a god was honored by you with a statue, which was erected in the river Tiber, between the two bridges, and bore this inscription in the Latin tongue, **Simoni Deo Sancto**, that is, **To Simon the Holy God.**

4. And nearly all the Samaritans and a

few even of other nations confess and worship him as the first God. And there went around with him at that time a certain Helena who had formerly been a prostitute in Tyre of Phœnicia; and her they call the first idea that proceeded from him.

5. Justin relates these things, and Irenæus also agrees with him in the first book of his work, Against Heresies, where he gives an account of the man and of his profane and impure teaching. It would be superfluous to quote his account here, for it is possible for those who wish to know the origin and the lives and the false doctrines of each of the heresiarchs that have followed him, as well as the customs practiced by them all, to find them treated at length in the above-mentioned work of Irenæus.

6. We have understood that Simon was the author of all heresy. From his time down to the present those who have followed his heresy have feigned the sober philosophy of the Christians, which

is celebrated among all on account of its purity of life. But they nevertheless have embraced again the superstitions of idols, which they seemed to have renounced; and they fall down before pictures and images of Simon himself and of the above-mentioned Helena who was with him; and they venture to worship them with incense and sacrifices and libations.

7. But those matters which they keep more secret than these, in regard to which they say that one upon first hearing them would be astonished, and, to use one of the written phrases in vogue among them, would be confounded, are in truth full of amazing things, and of madness and folly, being of such a sort that it is impossible not only to commit them to writing, but also for modest men even to utter them with the lips on account of their excessive baseness and lewdness.

8. For whatever could be conceived of, viler than the vilest thing – all that has been

outdone by this most abominable sect, which is composed of those who make a sport of those miserable females that are literally overwhelmed with all kinds of vices.

CHAPTER FOURTEEN

The Preaching of the Apostle Peter in Rome

1. THE EVIL POWER, who hates all that
is good and plots against the salvation of
men, constituted Simon at that time the
father and author of such wickedness, as
if to make him a mighty antagonist of the
great, inspired apostles of our Saviour.

2. For that divine and celestial grace
which co-operates with its ministers, by

their appearance and presence, quickly extinguished the kindled flame of evil, and humbled and cast down through them **"every high thing that exalted itself against the knowledge of God."** 2 Corinthians 10:5

3. Wherefore neither the conspiracy of Simon nor that of any of the others who arose at that period could accomplish anything in those apostolic times. For everything was conquered and subdued by the splendors of the truth and by the divine word itself which had but lately begun to shine from heaven upon men, and which was then flourishing upon earth, and dwelling in the apostles themselves.

4. Immediately the above-mentioned impostor was smitten in the eyes of his mind by a divine and miraculous flash, and after the evil deeds done by him had been first detected by the apostle Peter in Judea, he fled and made a great journey across the sea from the East to the West, thinking

that only thus could he live according to his mind.

5. And coming to the city of Rome, by the mighty co-operation of that power which was lying in wait there, he was in a short time so successful in his undertaking that those who dwelt there honored him as a god by the erection of a statue.

6. But this did not last long. For immediately, during the reign of Claudius, the all-good and gracious Providence, which watches over all things, led Peter, that strongest and greatest of the apostles, and the one who on account of his virtue was the speaker for all the others, to Rome against this great corrupter of life. Clad in divine armor like a noble commander of God, He carried the costly merchandise of the light of the understanding from the East to those who dwelt in the West, proclaiming the light itself, and the word which brings salvation to souls, and preaching the kingdom of heaven.

CHAPTER FIFTEEN

The Gospel according to Mark

1. AND THUS WHEN THE divine word had
made its home among them, the power
of Simon was quenched and immediately
destroyed, together with the man himself.
And so greatly did the splendor of piety
illumine the minds of Peter's hearers that
they were not satisfied with hearing once
only, and were not content with the unwritten
teaching of the divine Gospel, but with all
sorts of entreaties they besought Mark, a

follower of Peter, and the one whose Gospel is extant, that he would leave them a written monument of the doctrine which had been orally communicated to them. Nor did they cease until they had prevailed with the man, and had thus become the occasion of the written Gospel which bears the name of Mark.

2. And they say that Peter – when he had learned, through a revelation of the Spirit, of that which had been done – was pleased with the zeal of the men, and that the work obtained the sanction of his authority for the purpose of being used in the churches. Clement in the eighth book of his Hypotyposes gives this account, and with him agrees the bishop of Hierapolis named Papias. And Peter makes mention of Mark in his first epistle which they say that he wrote in Rome itself, as is indicated by him, when he calls the city, by a figure, Babylon, as he does in the following words: **"The church that is at Babylon, elected**

together with you, salutes you; and so does Marcus my son." 1 Peter 5:13

CHAPTER SIXTEEN

Mark first proclaimed
Christianity to the
Inhabitants of Egypt

1. AND THEY SAY THAT this Mark was
the first that was sent to Egypt, and that
he proclaimed the Gospel which he had
written, and first established churches in
Alexandria.

2. And the multitude of believers, both men

180

and women, that were collected there at the very outset, and lived lives of the most philosophical and excessive asceticism, was so great, that Philo thought it worth while to describe their pursuits, their meetings, their entertainments, and their whole manner of life.

CHAPTER SEVENTEEN

Philo's Account of the Ascetics of Egypt

1. IT IS ALSO SAID that Philo in the reign of Claudius became acquainted at Rome with Peter, who was then preaching there. Nor is this indeed improbable, for the work of which we have spoken, and which was composed by him some years later, clearly contains those rules of the Church which are even to this day observed among us.

2. And since he describes as accurately as possible the life of our ascetics, it is clear that he not only knew, but that he also approved, while he venerated and extolled, the apostolic men of his time, who were as it seems of the Hebrew race, and hence observed, after the manner of the Jews, the most of the customs of the ancients.

3. In the work to which he gave the title, **On a Contemplative Life or on Suppliants**, after affirming in the first place that he will add to those things which he is about to relate nothing contrary to truth or of his own invention, he says that these men were called Therapeutæ and the women that were with them Therapeutrides. He then adds the reasons for such a name, explaining it from the fact that they applied remedies and healed the souls of those who came to them, by relieving them like physicians, of evil passions, or from the fact that they served and worshipped the Deity in purity and sincerity.

183

4. Whether Philo himself gave them this name, employing an epithet well suited to their mode of life, or whether the first of them really called themselves so in the beginning, since the name of Christians was not yet everywhere known, we need not discuss here.

5. He bears witness, however, that first of all they renounce their property. When they begin the philosophical mode of life, he says, they give up their goods to their relatives, and then, renouncing all the cares of life, they go forth beyond the walls and dwell in lonely fields and gardens, knowing well that intercourse with people of a different character is unprofitable and harmful. They did this at that time, as seems probable, under the influence of a spirited and ardent faith, practicing in emulation the prophets' mode of life.

6. For in the Acts of the Apostles, a work universally acknowledged as authentic, it is recorded that all the companions of the

apostles sold their possessions and their property and distributed to all according to the necessity of each one, so that no one among them was in want. **"For as many as were possessors of lands or houses,"** as the account says, **"sold them and brought the prices of the things that were sold, and laid them at the apostles' feet, so that distribution was made unto every man according as he had need."** Acts 2:45

7. Philo bears witness to facts very much like those here described and then adds the following account: Everywhere in the world is this race found. For it was fitting that both Greek and Barbarian should share in what is perfectly good. But the race particularly abounds in Egypt, in each of its so-called **nomes**, and especially about Alexandria.

8. The best men from every quarter emigrate, as if to a colony of the Therapeutæ's fatherland, to a certain very suitable spot which lies above the Lake

Maria upon a low hill excellently situated on account of its security and the mildness of the atmosphere.

9. And then a little further on, after describing the kind of houses which they had, he speaks as follows concerning their churches, which were scattered about here and there: **"In each house there is a sacred apartment which is called a sanctuary and monastery, where, quite alone, they perform the mysteries of the religious life. They bring nothing into it, neither drink nor food, nor any of the other things which contribute to the necessities of the body, but only the laws, and the inspired oracles of the prophets, and hymns and such other things as augment and make perfect their knowledge and piety."**

10. And after some other matters he says: The whole interval, from morning to evening, is for them a time of exercise. For they read the holy Scriptures, and explain the philosophy of their fathers in an

allegorical manner, regarding the written words as symbols of hidden truth which is communicated in obscure figures.

11. They have also writings of ancient men, who were the founders of their sect, and who left many monuments of the allegorical method. These they use as models, and imitate their principles.

12. These things seem to have been stated by a man who had heard them expounding their sacred writings. But it is highly probable that the works of the ancients, which he says they had, were the Gospels and the writings of the apostles, and probably some expositions of the ancient prophets, such as are contained in the Epistle to the Hebrews, and in many others of Paul's Epistles.

13. Then again he writes as follows concerning the new psalms which they composed: **"So that they not only spend their time in meditation, but they also compose songs and hymns to God in every variety of metre and melody,**

though they divide them, of course, into measures of more than common solemnity."

14. The same book contains an account of many other things, but it seemed necessary to select those facts which exhibit the characteristics of the ecclesiastical mode of life.

15. But if any one thinks that what has been said is not peculiar to the Gospel polity, but that it can be applied to others besides those mentioned, let him be convinced by the subsequent words of the same author, in which, if he is unprejudiced, he will find undisputed testimony on this subject. Philo's words are as follows:

16. Having laid down temperance as a sort of foundation in the soul, they build upon it the other virtues. None of them may take food or drink before sunset, since they regard philosophizing as a work worthy of the light, but attention to the wants of the body as proper only in the darkness, and

therefore assign the day to the former, but to the latter a small portion of the night.

17. But some, in whom a great desire for knowledge dwells, forget to take food for three days; and some are so delighted and feast so luxuriously upon wisdom, which furnishes doctrines richly and without stint, that they abstain even twice as long as this, and are accustomed, after six days, scarcely to take necessary food. These statements of Philo we regard as referring clearly and indisputably to those of our communion.

18. But if after these things any one still obstinately persists in denying the reference, let him renounce his incredulity and be convinced by yet more striking examples, which are to be found nowhere else than in the evangelical religion of the Christians.

19. For they say that there were women also with those of whom we are speaking, and that the most of them were aged virgins who had preserved their chastity, not out

of necessity, as some of the priestesses among the Greeks, but rather by their own choice, through zeal and a desire for wisdom. And that in their earnest desire to live with it as their companion they paid no attention to the pleasures of the body, seeking not mortal but immortal progeny, which only the pious soul is able to bear of itself.

20. Then after a little he adds still more emphatically: **"They expound the Sacred Scriptures figuratively by means of allegories. For the whole law seems to these men to resemble a living organism, of which the spoken words constitute the body, while the hidden sense stored up within the words constitutes the soul. This hidden meaning has first been particularly studied by this sect, which sees, revealed as in a mirror of names, the surpassing beauties of the thoughts."**

21. Why is it necessary to add to these things their meetings and the respective

occupations of the men and of the women during those meetings, and the practices which are even to the present day habitually observed by us, especially such as we are accustomed to observe at the feast of the Saviour's passion, with fasting and night watching and study of the divine Word.

22. These things the above-mentioned author has related in his own work, indicating a mode of life which has been preserved to the present time by us alone, recording especially the vigils kept in connection with the great festival, and the exercises performed during those vigils, and the hymns customarily recited by us, and describing how, while one sings regularly in time, the others listen in silence, and join in chanting only the close of the hymns; and how, on the days referred to they sleep on the ground on beds of straw, and to use his own words, **"taste no wine at all, nor any flesh, but water is their only drink, and the reish with their bread is salt and**

191

hyssop."

23. In addition to this Philo describes the order of dignities which exists among those who carry on the services of the church, mentioning the diaconate, and the office of bishop, which takes the precedence over all the others. But whosoever desires a more accurate knowledge of these matters may get it from the history already cited.

24. But that Philo, when he wrote these things, had in view the first heralds of the Gospel and the customs handed down from the beginning by the apostles, is clear to every one.

CHAPTER EIGHTEEN

The Works of Philo that have come down to us

1. COPIOUS IN LANGUAGE, comprehensive in thought, sublime and elevated in his views of divine Scripture, Philo has produced manifold and various expositions of the sacred books. On the one hand, he expounds in order the events recorded in Genesis in the books to which he gives the title **Allegories of the Sacred Laws**; on the

other hand, he makes successive divisions of
the chapters in the Scriptures which are the
subject of investigation, and gives objections
and solutions, in the books which he quite
suitably calls **Questions and Answers on
Genesis and Exodus**.

2. There are, besides these, treatises
expressly worked out by him on
certain subjects, such as the two
books **On Agriculture**, and the same
number **On Drunkenness**; and some
others distinguished by different titles
corresponding to the contents of each; for
instance, **Concerning the Things Which
the Sober Mind Desires and Execrates**,
On the Confusion of Tongues, **On Flight
and Discovery**, **On Assembly for the
Sake of Instruction**, **On the Question,
'Who is Heir to Things Divine?'** or **On
the Division of Things into Equal and
Unequal**, and still further the work **On the
Three Virtues Which With Others Have
Been Described by Moses**.

3. In addition to these is the work **On Those Whose Names Have Been Changed and Why They Have Been Changed**, in which he says that he had written also two books **On Covenants.**

4. And there is also a work of his **On Emigration**, and one **On the Life of a Wise Man Made Perfect in Righteousness**, or **On Unwritten Laws;** and still further the work **On Giants** or **On the Immutability of God**, and a first, second, third, fourth and fifth book **On the Proposition, That Dreams According to Moses are Sent by God.** These are the books on Genesis that have come down to us.

5. But on Exodus we are acquainted with the first, second, third, fourth and fifth books of **Questions and Answers;** also with that **On the Tabernacle**, and that **On the Ten Commandments**, and the four books **On the Laws Which Refer Especially to the Principal Divisions of the Ten Commandments**, and another **On Animals**

Intended for Sacrifice and **On the Kinds of Sacrifice**, and another **On the Rewards Fixed in the Law for the Good, and on the Punishments and Curses Fixed for the Wicked.**

6. In addition to all these there are extant also some single-volumed works of his; as for instance, the work **On Providence**, and the book composed by him **On the Jews**, and **The Statesman**; and still further, **Alexander**, or **On the Possession of Reason by the Irrational Animals.** Besides these there is a work **On the Proposition that Every Wicked Man is a Slave**, to which is subjoined the work **On the Proposition that Every Good Man is Free.**

7. After these was composed by him the work **On the Contemplative Life**, or **On Suppliants**, from which we have drawn the facts concerning the life of the apostolic men; and still further, the **Interpretation of the Hebrew Names in the Law and in the**

Prophets are said to be the result of his industry.

8. And he is said to have read in the presence of the whole Roman Senate during the reign of Claudius the work which he had written, when he came to Rome under Caius, concerning Caius' hatred of the gods, and to which, with ironical reference to its character, he had given the title **On the Virtues**. And his discourses were so much admired as to be deemed worthy of a place in the libraries.

9. At this time, while Paul was completing his journey **"from Jerusalem and round about unto Illyricum,"** Romans 15:19 Claudius drove the Jews out of Rome; and Aquila and Priscilla, leaving Rome with the other Jews, came to Asia, and there abode with the apostle Paul, who was confirming the churches of that region whose foundations he had newly laid. The sacred book of the Acts informs us also of these things.

CHAPTER NINETEEN

The Calamity which befell the Jews in Jerusalem on the Day of the Passover

1. WHILE CLAUDIUS WAS STILL emperor, it happened that so great a tumult and disturbance took place in Jerusalem at the feast of the Passover, that thirty thousand of those Jews alone who were forcibly crowded together at the gate of the temple

perished, being trampled under foot by one another. Thus the festival became a season of mourning for all the nation, and there was weeping in every house. These things are related literally by Josephus.

2. But Claudius appointed Agrippa, son of Agrippa, king of the Jews, having sent Felix as procurator of the whole country of Samaria and Galilee, and of the land called Perea. And after he had reigned thirteen years and eight months he died, and left Nero as his successor in the empire.

CHAPTER TWENTY

The Events which took Place in Jerusalem during the Reign of Nero

1. JOSEPHUS AGAIN, in the twentieth book of his Antiquities, relates the quarrel which arose among the priests during the reign of Nero, while Felix was procurator of Judea.

2. His words are as follows : There arose a quarrel between the high priests on the

one hand and the priests and leaders of the people of Jerusalem on the other. And each of them collected a body of the boldest and most restless men, and put himself at their head, and whenever they met they hurled invectives and stones at each other. And there was no one that would interpose; but these things were done at will as if in a city destitute of a ruler.

3. And so great was the shamelessness and audacity of the high priests that they dared to send their servants to the threshing-floors to seize the tithes due to the priests; and thus those of the priests that were poor were seen to be perishing of want. In this way did the violence of the factions prevail over all justice.

4. And the same author again relates that about the same time there sprang up in Jerusalem a certain kind of robbers, **"who by day,"** as he says, **"and in the middle of the city slew those who met them."**

5. For, especially at the feasts, they

mingled with the multitude, and with short swords, which they concealed under their garments, they stabbed the most distinguished men. And when they fell, the murderers themselves were among those who expressed their indignation. And thus on account of the confidence which was reposed in them by all, they remained undiscovered.

6. The first that was slain by them was Jonathan the high priest; and after him many were killed every day, until the fear became worse than the evil itself, each one, as in battle, hourly expecting death.

CHAPTER TWENTY ONE

The Egyptian, who is mentioned also in the Acts of the Apostles

1. AFTER OTHER MATTERS HE proceeds as follows: But the Jews were afflicted with a greater plague than these by the Egyptian false prophet. For there appeared in the land an impostor who aroused faith in himself as a prophet, and collected about thirty thousand

of those whom he had deceived, and led them from the desert to the so-called Mount of Olives whence he was prepared to enter Jerusalem by force and to overpower the Roman garrison and seize the government of the people, using those who made the attack with him as body guards.

2. But Felix anticipated his attack, and went out to meet him with the Roman legionaries, and all the people joined in the defense, so that when the battle was fought the Egyptian fled with a few followers, but the most of them were destroyed or taken captive.

3. Josephus relates these events in the second book of his History. But it is worth while comparing the account of the Egyptian given here with that contained in the Acts of the Apostles. In the time of Felix it was said to Paul by the centurion in Jerusalem, when the multitude of the Jews raised a disturbance against the apostle, **"Are you not he who before these days**

made an uproar, and led out into the wilderness four thousand men that were murderers?" Acts 21:38 These are the events which took place in the time of Felix.

CHAPTER TWENTY TWO

Paul having been sent bound from Judea to Rome, made his Defense, and was acquitted of every Charge

1. FESTUS WAS SENT BY Nero to be Felix's successor. Under him Paul, having made his defense, was sent bound to Rome. Aristarchus was with him, whom he also somewhere in his epistles quite naturally

calls his fellow-prisoner. Colossians 4:10 And Luke, who wrote the Acts of the Apostles, brought his history to a close at this point, after stating that Paul spent two whole years at Rome as a prisoner at large, and preached the word of God without restraint.

2. Thus after he had made his defense it is said that the apostle was sent again upon the ministry of preaching, and that upon coming to the same city a second time he suffered martyrdom. In this imprisonment he wrote his second epistle to Timothy, in which he mentions his first defense and his impending death.

3. But hear his testimony on these matters: **"At my first answer,"** he says, **"no man stood with me, but all men forsook me: I pray God that it may not be laid to their charge. Notwithstanding the Lord stood with me, and strengthened me; that by me the preaching might be fully known, and that all the Gentiles might hear: and I was delivered out of the mouth of the**

lion." 2 Timothy 4:16-17

4. He plainly indicates in these words that on the former occasion, in order that the preaching might be fulfilled by him, he was rescued from the mouth of the lion, referring, in this expression, to Nero, as is probable on account of the latter's cruelty. He did not therefore afterward add the similar statement, **"He will rescue me from the mouth of the lion"**; for he saw in the spirit that his end would not be long delayed.

5. Wherefore he adds to the words, **"And he delivered me from the mouth of the lion,"** this sentence: **"The Lord shall deliver me from every evil work, and will preserve me unto his heavenly kingdom,"** 2 Timothy 4:18 indicating his speedy martyrdom; which he also foretells still more clearly in the same epistle, when he writes, **"For I am now ready to be offered, and the time of my departure is at hand."**

6. In his second epistle to Timothy, moreover, he indicates that Luke was with him when he wrote, but at his first defense not even he. Whence it is probable that Luke wrote the Acts of the Apostles at that time, continuing his history down to the period when he was with Paul.

7. But these things have been adduced by us to show that Paul's martyrdom did not take place at the time of that Roman sojourn which Luke records.

8. It is probable indeed that as Nero was more disposed to mildness in the beginning, Paul's defense of his doctrine was more easily received; but that when he had advanced to the commission of lawless deeds of daring, he made the apostles as well as others the subjects of his attacks.

CHAPTER TWENTY THREE

The Martyrdom of James, who was called the Brother of the Lord

1. BUT AFTER PAUL, in consequence of his appeal to Cæsar, had been sent to Rome by Festus, the Jews, being frustrated in their hope of entrapping him by the snares which they had laid for him, turned against James, the brother of the Lord, to whom

the episcopal seat at Jerusalem had been entrusted by the apostles. The following daring measures were undertaken by them against him.

2. Leading him into their midst they demanded of him that he should renounce faith in Christ in the presence of all the people. But, contrary to the opinion of all, with a clear voice, and with greater boldness than they had anticipated, he spoke out before the whole multitude and confessed that our Saviour and Lord Jesus is the Son of God. But they were unable to bear longer the testimony of the man who, on account of the excellence of ascetic virtue and of piety which he exhibited in his life, was esteemed by all as the most just of men, and consequently they slew him. Opportunity for this deed of violence was furnished by the prevailing anarchy, which was caused by the fact that Festus had died just at this time in Judea, and that the province was thus without a governor

and head.

3. The manner of James' death has been already indicated by the above-quoted words of Clement, who records that he was thrown from the pinnacle of the temple, and was beaten to death with a club. But Hegesippus, who lived immediately after the apostles, gives the most accurate account in the fifth book of his Memoirs. He writes as follows:

4. James, the brother of the Lord, succeeded to the government of the Church in conjunction with the apostles. He has been called the Just by all from the time of our Saviour to the present day; for there were many that bore the name of James.

5. He was holy from his mother's womb; and he drank no wine nor strong drink, nor did he eat flesh. No razor came upon his head; he did not anoint himself with oil, and he did not use the bath.

6. He alone was permitted to enter into the holy place; for he wore not woolen but

linen garments. And he was in the habit of entering alone into the temple, and was frequently found upon his knees begging forgiveness for the people, so that his knees became hard like those of a camel, in consequence of his constantly bending them in his worship of God, and asking forgiveness for the people.

7. Because of his exceeding great justice he was called the Just, and Oblias, which signifies in Greek, 'Bulwark of the people' and 'Justice,' in accordance with what the prophets declare concerning him.

8. Now some of the seven sects, which existed among the people and which have been mentioned by me in the Memoirs, asked him, 'What is the gate of Jesus?' and he replied that he was the Saviour.

9. On account of these words some believed that Jesus is the Christ. But the sects mentioned above did not believe either in a resurrection or in one's coming to give to every man according to his works. But

as many as believed did so on account of James.

10. Therefore when many even of the rulers believed, there was a commotion among the Jews and Scribes and Pharisees, who said that there was danger that the whole people would be looking for Jesus as the Christ. Coming therefore in a body to James they said, 'We entreat you, restrain the people; for they are gone astray in regard to Jesus, as if he were the Christ. We entreat you to persuade all that have come to the feast of the Passover concerning Jesus; for we all have confidence in you. For we bear you witness, as do all the people, that you are just, and do not respect persons. Matthew 22:16

11. Therefore, persuade the multitude not to be led astray concerning Jesus. For the whole people, and all of us also, have confidence in you. Stand therefore upon the pinnacle of the temple, that from that high position you may be clearly seen, and that

your words may be readily heard by all the people. For all the tribes, with the Gentiles also, have come together on account of the Passover.'

12. The aforesaid Scribes and Pharisees therefore placed James upon the pinnacle of the temple, and cried out to him and said: 'You just one, in whom we ought all to have confidence, forasmuch as the people are led astray after Jesus, the crucified one, declare to us, what is the gate of Jesus.'

13. And he answered with a loud voice, 'Why do you ask me concerning Jesus, the Son of Man? He himself sits in heaven at the right hand of the great Power, and is about to come upon the clouds of heaven.'

14. And when many were fully convinced and gloried in the testimony of James, and said, 'Hosanna to the Son of David,' these same Scribes and Pharisees said again to one another, 'We have done badly in supplying such testimony to Jesus. But let us go up and throw him down, in order that

they may be afraid to believe him.'

15. And they cried out, saying, 'Oh! Oh! The just man is also in error.' And they fulfilled the Scripture written in Isaiah, 'Let us take away the just man, because he is troublesome to us: therefore they shall eat the fruit of their doings.'

16. So they went up and threw down the just man, and said to each other, 'Let us stone James the Just.' And they began to stone him, for he was not killed by the fall; but he turned and knelt down and said, 'I entreat you, Lord God our Father, forgive them, for they know not what they do.' Luke 23:34

17. And while they were thus stoning him one of the priests of the sons of Rechab, the son of the Rechabites, who are mentioned by Jeremiah the prophet, cried out, saying, 'Stop. What are you doing? The just one prays for you.'

18. And one of them, who was a fuller, took the club with which he beat out clothes

and struck the just man on the head. And thus he suffered martyrdom. And they buried him on the spot, by the temple, and his monument still remains by the temple. He became a true witness, both to Jews and Greeks, that Jesus is the Christ. And immediately Vespasian besieged them.

19. These things are related at length by Hegesippus, who is in agreement with Clement. James was so admirable a man and so celebrated among all for his justice, that the more sensible even of the Jews were of the opinion that this was the cause of the siege of Jerusalem, which happened to them immediately after his martyrdom for no other reason than their daring act against him.

20. Josephus, at least, has not hesitated to testify this in his writings, where he says, **"These things happened to the Jews to avenge James the Just, who was a brother of Jesus, that is called the Christ. For the Jews slew him, although he was**

a most just man."

21. And the same writer records his death also in the twentieth book of his Antiquities in the following words: But the emperor, when he learned of the death of Festus, sent Albinus to be procurator of Judea. But the younger Ananus, who, as we have already said, had obtained the high priesthood, was of an exceedingly bold and reckless disposition. He belonged, moreover, to the sect of the Sadducees, who are the most cruel of all the Jews in the execution of judgment, as we have already shown.

22. Ananus, therefore, being of this character, and supposing that he had a favorable opportunity on account of the fact that Festus was dead, and Albinus was still on the way, called together the Sanhedrin, and brought before them the brother of Jesus, the so-called Christ, James by name, together with some others, and accused them of violating the law, and condemned them to be stoned.

23. But those in the city who seemed most moderate and skilled in the law were very angry at this, and sent secretly to the king, requesting him to order Ananus to cease such proceedings. For he had not done right even this first time. And certain of them also went to meet Albinus, who was journeying from Alexandria, and reminded him that it was not lawful for Ananus to summon the Sanhedrin without his knowledge.

24. And Albinus, being persuaded by their representations, wrote in anger to Ananus, threatening him with punishment. And the king, Agrippa, in consequence, deprived him of the high priesthood, which he had held three months, and appointed Jesus, the son of Damnæus.

25. These things are recorded in regard to James, who is said to be the author of the first of the so-called catholic epistles. But it is to be observed that it is disputed; at least, not many of the ancients have mentioned it, as is the case likewise with the epistle

that bears the name of Jude, which is also one of the seven so-called catholic epistles. Nevertheless we know that these also, with the rest, have been read publicly in very many churches.

CHAPTER TWENTY FOUR

Annianus the First Bishop of the Church of Alexandria after Mark

1. WHEN NERO WAS IN the eighth year of his reign, Annianus succeeded Mark the Evangelist in the administration of the parish of Alexandria.

CHAPTER TWENTY FIVE

The Persecution under Nero in which Paul and Peter were honored at Rome with Martyrdom in Behalf of Religion

1. WHEN THE GOVERNMENT OF Nero was now firmly established, he began to plunge into unholy pursuits, and armed himself even against the religion of the God of the universe.

2. To describe the greatness of his depravity does not lie within the plan of the present work. As there are many indeed that have recorded his history in most accurate narratives, every one may at his pleasure learn from them the coarseness of the man's extraordinary madness, under the influence of which, after he had accomplished the destruction of so many myriads without any reason, he ran into such blood-guiltiness that he did not spare even his nearest relatives and dearest friends, but destroyed his mother and his brothers and his wife, with very many others of his own family as he would private and public enemies, with various kinds of deaths.

3. But with all these things this particular in the catalogue of his crimes was still wanting, that he was the first of the emperors who showed himself an enemy of the divine religion.

4. The Roman Tertullian is likewise a witness of this. He writes as follows: "**Examine your**

records. There you will find that Nero was the first that persecuted this doctrine, particularly then when after subduing all the east, he exercised his cruelty against all at Rome. We glory in having such a man the leader in our punishment. For whoever knows him can understand that nothing was condemned by Nero unless it was something of great excellence."

5. Thus publicly announcing himself as the first among God's chief enemies, he was led on to the slaughter of the apostles. It is, therefore, recorded that Paul was beheaded in Rome itself, and that Peter likewise was crucified under Nero. This account of Peter and Paul is substantiated by the fact that their names are preserved in the cemeteries of that place even to the present day.

6. It is confirmed likewise by Caius, a member of the Church, who arose under Zephyrinus, bishop of Rome. He, in a published disputation with Proclus, the leader of the Phrygian heresy, speaks as

follows concerning the places where the sacred corpses of the aforesaid apostles are laid:

7. **"But I can show the trophies of the apostles. For if you will go to the Vatican or to the Ostian way, you will find the trophies of those who laid the foundations of this church."**

8. And that they both suffered martyrdom at the same time is stated by Dionysius, bishop of Corinth, in his epistle to the Romans, in the following words: **"You have thus by such an admonition bound together the planting of Peter and of Paul at Rome and Corinth. For both of them planted and likewise taught us in our Corinth. And they taught together in like manner in Italy, and suffered martyrdom at the same time."** I have quoted these things in order that the truth of the history might be still more confirmed.

CHAPTER TWENTY SIX

The Jews, afflicted with Innumerable Evils, commenced the Last War Against the Romans

1. JOSEPHUS AGAIN, after relating many things in connection with the calamity which came upon the whole Jewish nation, records, in addition to many other circumstances, that a great many of the most honorable among

the Jews were scourged in Jerusalem itself and then crucified by Florus. It happened that he was procurator of Judea when the war began to be kindled, in the twelfth year of Nero.

2. Josephus says that at that time a terrible commotion was stirred up throughout all Syria in consequence of the revolt of the Jews, and that everywhere the latter were destroyed without mercy, like enemies, by the inhabitants of the cities, **"so that one could see cities filled with unburied corpses, and the dead bodies of the aged scattered about with the bodies of infants, and women without even a covering for their nakedness, and the whole province full of indescribable calamities, while the dread of those things that were threatened was greater than the sufferings themselves which they anywhere endured."** Such is the account of Josephus; and such was the condition of the Jews at that time.

BOOK THREE

CHAPTER ONE

The Parts of the World in which the Apostles preached Christ

1. SUCH WAS THE CONDITION of the Jews. Meanwhile the holy apostles and disciples of our Saviour were dispersed throughout the world. Parthia, according

to tradition, was allotted to Thomas as his field of labor, Scythia to Andrew, and Asia to John, who, after he had lived some time there, died at Ephesus.

2. Peter appears to have preached in Pontus, Galatia, Bithynia, Cappadocia, and Asia to the Jews of the dispersion. And at last, having come to Rome, he was crucified head-downwards; for he had requested that he might suffer in this way. What do we need to say concerning Paul, who preached the Gospel of Christ from Jerusalem to Illyricum, and afterwards suffered martyrdom in Rome under Nero? These facts are related by Origen in the third volume of his Commentary on Genesis.

CHAPTER TWO

The First Successor to St. Peter in Rome

1. AFTER THE MARTYRDOM OF Paul and of Peter, Linus was the first to obtain the episcopate of the church at Rome. Paul mentions him, when writing to Timothy from Rome, in the salutation at the end of the epistle.

CHAPTER THREE

The Epistles of the Apostles

1. ONE EPISTLE OF PETER, that called the first, is acknowledged as genuine. And this the ancient elders used freely in their own writings as an undisputed work. But we have learned that his extant second Epistle does not belong to the canon; yet, as it has appeared profitable to many, it has been used with the other Scriptures.

2. The so-called Acts of Peter, however,

and the Gospel which bears his name, and the Preaching and the Apocalypse, as they are called, we know have not been universally accepted, because no ecclesiastical writer, ancient or modern, has made use of testimonies drawn from them.

3. But in the course of my history I shall be careful to show, in addition to the official succession, what ecclesiastical writers have from time to time made use of any of the disputed works, and what they have said in regard to the canonical and accepted writings, as well as in regard to those which are not of this class.

4. Such are the writings that bear the name of Peter, only one of which I know to be genuine and acknowledged by the ancient elders.

5. Paul's fourteen epistles are well known and undisputed. It is not indeed right to overlook the fact that some have rejected the Epistle to the Hebrews, saying that it

is disputed by the church of Rome, on the ground that it was not written by Paul. But what has been said concerning this epistle by those who lived before our time I shall quote in the proper place. In regard to the so-called Acts of Paul, I have not found them among the undisputed writings.

6. But as the same apostle, in the salutations at the end of the Epistle to the Romans, has made mention among others of Hermas, to whom the book called The Shepherd is ascribed, it should be observed that this too has been disputed by some, and on their account cannot be placed among the acknowledged books; while by others it is considered quite indispensable, especially to those who need instruction in the elements of the faith. Hence, as we know, it has been publicly read in churches, and I have found that some of the most ancient writers used it.

7. This will serve to show the divine writings that are undisputed as well as those that are not universally acknowledged.

CHAPTER FOUR

The First Successors of the Apostles

1. THAT PAUL PREACHED TO the Gentiles and laid the foundations of the churches **"from Jerusalem round about even unto Illyricum,"** is evident both from his own words, Romans 15:19 and from the account which Luke has given in the Acts.

2. And in how many provinces Peter preached Christ and taught the doctrine of

the new covenant to those of the circumcision is clear from his own words in his epistle already mentioned as undisputed, in which he writes to the Hebrews of the dispersion in Pontus, Galatia, Cappadocia, Asia, and Bithynia. 1 Peter 1:1

3. But the number and the names of those among them that became true and zealous followers of the apostles, and were judged worthy to tend the churches founded by them, it is not easy to tell, except those mentioned in the writings of Paul.

4. For he had innumerable fellow-laborers, or **"fellow-soldiers,"** as he called them, and most of them were honored by him with an imperishable memorial, for he gave enduring testimony concerning them in his own epistles.

5. Luke also in the Acts speaks of his friends, and mentions them by name.

6. Timothy, so it is recorded, was the first to receive the episcopate of the parish in Ephesus, Titus of the churches in Crete.

7. But Luke, who was of Antiochian parentage and a physician by profession, and who was especially intimate with Paul and well acquainted with the rest of the apostles, has left us, in two inspired books, proofs of that spiritual healing art which he learned from them. One of these books is the Gospel, which he testifies that he wrote as those who were from the beginning eyewitnesses and ministers of the word delivered unto him, all of whom, as he says, he followed accurately from the first. Luke 1:2-3 The other book is the Acts of the Apostles which he composed not from the accounts of others, but from what he had seen himself.

8. And they say that Paul meant to refer to Luke's Gospel wherever, as if speaking of some gospel of his own, he used the words, **"according to my Gospel."**

9. As to the rest of his followers, Paul testifies that Crescens was sent to Gaul; but Linus, whom he mentions in the Second

Epistle to Timothy 2 Timothy 4:21 as his companion at Rome, was Peter's successor in the episcopate of the church there, as has already been shown.

10. Clement also, who was appointed third bishop of the church at Rome, was, as Paul testifies, his co-laborer and fellow-soldier.

11. Besides these, that Areopagite, named Dionysius, who was the first to believe after Paul's address to the Athenians in the Areopagus (as recorded by Luke in the Acts) is mentioned by another Dionysius, an ancient writer and pastor of the parish in Corinth, as the first bishop of the church at Athens.

12. But the events connected with the apostolic succession we shall relate at the proper time. Meanwhile let us continue the course of our history.

CHAPTER FIVE

The Last Siege of the Jews after Christ

1. AFTER NERO HAD HELD the power thirteen years, and Galba and Otho had ruled a year and six months, Vespasian, who had become distinguished in the campaigns against the Jews, was proclaimed sovereign in Judea and received the title of Emperor from the armies there. Setting out immediately, therefore, for Rome, he

entrusted the conduct of the war against the Jews to his son Titus.

2. For the Jews after the ascension of our Saviour, in addition to their crime against him, had been devising as many plots as they could against his apostles. First Stephen was stoned to death by them, and after him James, the son of Zebedee and the brother of John, was beheaded, and finally James, the first that had obtained the episcopal seat in Jerusalem after the ascension of our Saviour, died in the manner already described. But the rest of the apostles, who had been incessantly plotted against with a view to their destruction, and had been driven out of the land of Judea, went unto all nations to preach the Gospel, relying upon the power of Christ, who had said to them, **"Go and make disciples of all the nations in my name."**

3. But the people of the church in Jerusalem had been commanded by a revelation, vouchsafed to approved men there before

the war, to leave the city and to dwell in a certain town of Perea called Pella. And when those that believed in Christ had come there from Jerusalem, then, as if the royal city of the Jews and the whole land of Judea were entirely destitute of holy men, the judgment of God at length overtook those who had committed such outrages against Christ and his apostles, and totally destroyed that generation of impious men.

4. But the number of calamities which everywhere fell upon the nation at that time; the extreme misfortunes to which the inhabitants of Judea were especially subjected, the thousands of men, as well as women and children, that perished by the sword, by famine, and by other forms of death innumerable – all these things, as well as the many great sieges which were carried on against the cities of Judea, and the excessive sufferings endured by those that fled to Jerusalem itself, as to a city of perfect safety, and finally the general course

of the whole war, as well as its particular occurrences in detail, and how at last the abomination of desolation, proclaimed by the prophets, Daniel 9:27 stood in the very temple of God, so celebrated of old, the temple which was now awaiting its total and final destruction by fire – all these things any one that wishes may find accurately described in the history written by Josephus.

5. But it is necessary to state that this writer records that the multitude of those who were assembled from all Judea at the time of the Passover, to the number of three million souls, were shut up in Jerusalem **"as in a prison,"** to use his own words.

6. For it was right that in the very days in which they had inflicted suffering upon the Saviour and the Benefactor of all, the Christ of God, that in those days, shut up **"as in a prison,"** they should meet with destruction at the hands of divine justice.

7. But passing by the particular calamities

which they suffered from the attempts made upon them by the sword and by other means, I think it necessary to relate only the misfortunes which the famine caused, that those who read this work may have some means of knowing that God was not long in executing vengeance upon them for their wickedness against the Christ of God.

CHAPTER SIX

The Famine which oppressed them

1. TAKING THE FIFTH BOOK of the History of Josephus again in our hands, let us go through the tragedy of events which then occurred.

2. **"For the wealthy,"** he says, it was equally dangerous to remain. For under pretense that they were going to desert, men were put to death for their wealth. The madness of the

243

seditions increased with the famine and both the miseries were inflamed more and more day by day.

3. Nowhere was food to be seen; but, bursting into the houses men searched them thoroughly, and whenever they found anything to eat they tormented the owners on the ground that they had denied that they had anything; but if they found nothing, they tortured them on the ground that they had more carefully concealed it.

4. The proof of their having or not having food was found in the bodies of the poor wretches. Those of them who were still in good condition they assumed were well supplied with food, while those who were already wasted away they passed by, for it seemed absurd to slay those who were on the point of perishing for want.

5. Many, indeed, secretly sold their possessions for one measure of wheat, if they belonged to the wealthier class, of barley if they were poorer. Then shutting themselves

up in the innermost parts of their houses, some ate the grain uncooked on account of their terrible want, while others baked it according as necessity and fear dictated.

6. Nowhere were tables set, but, snatching the yet uncooked food from the fire, they tore it in pieces. Wretched was the fare, and a lamentable spectacle it was to see the more powerful secure an abundance while the weaker mourned.

7. Of all evils, indeed, famine is the worst, and it destroys nothing so effectively as shame. For that which under other circumstances is worthy of respect, in the midst of famine is despised. Thus women snatched the food from the very mouths of their husbands and children, from their fathers, and what was most pitiable of all, mothers from their babes. And while their dearest ones were wasting away in their arms, they were not ashamed to take away from them the last drops that supported life.

8. And even while they were eating thus they

did not remain undiscovered. But everywhere the rioters appeared, to rob them even of these portions of food. For whenever they saw a house shut up, they regarded it as a sign that those inside were taking food. And immediately bursting open the doors they rushed in and seized what they were eating, almost forcing it out of their very throats.

9. Old men who clung to their food were beaten, and if the women concealed it in their hands, their hair was torn for so doing. There was pity neither for gray hairs nor for infants, but, taking up the babes that clung to their morsels of food, they dashed them to the ground. But to those that anticipated their entrance and swallowed what they were about to seize, they were still more cruel, just as if they had been wronged by them.

10. And they devised the most terrible modes of torture to discover food, stopping up the privy passages of the poor wretches with bitter herbs, and piercing their seats with

sharp rods. And men suffered things horrible even to hear of, for the sake of compelling them to confess to the possession of one loaf of bread, or in order that they might be made to disclose a single drachm of barley which they had concealed. But the tormentors themselves did not suffer hunger.

11. Their conduct might indeed have seemed less barbarous if they had been driven to it by necessity; but they did it for the sake of exercising their madness and of providing sustenance for themselves for days to come.

12. And when any one crept out of the city by night as far as the outposts of the Romans to collect wild herbs and grass, they went to meet him; and when he thought he had already escaped the enemy, they seized what he had brought with him, and even though oftentimes the man would entreat them, and, calling upon the most awful name of God, adjure them to give him a portion of what he had obtained at the risk of his life,

they would give him nothing back. Indeed, it was fortunate if the one that was plundered was not also slain.

13. To this account Josephus, after relating other things, adds the following: The possibility of going out of the city being brought to an end, all hope of safety for the Jews was cut off. And the famine increased and devoured the people by houses and families. And the rooms were filled with dead women and children, the lanes of the city with the corpses of old men.

14. Children and youths, swollen with the famine, wandered about the marketplaces like shadows, and fell down wherever the death agony overtook them. The sick were not strong enough to bury even their own relatives, and those who had the strength hesitated because of the multitude of the dead and the uncertainty as to their own fate. Many, indeed, died while they were burying others, and many betook themselves to their graves before death came upon them.

15. There was neither weeping nor lamentation under these misfortunes; but the famine stifled the natural affections. Those that were dying a lingering death looked with dry eyes upon those that had gone to their rest before them. Deep silence and death-laden night encircled the city.

16. But the robbers were more terrible than these miseries; for they broke open the houses, which were now mere sepulchres, robbed the dead and stripped the covering from their bodies, and went away with a laugh. They tried the points of their swords in the dead bodies, and some that were lying on the ground still alive they thrust through in order to test their weapons. But those that prayed that they would use their right hand and their sword upon them, they contemptuously left to be destroyed by the famine. Every one of these died with eyes fixed upon the temple; and they left the seditious alive.

17. These at first gave orders that the dead should be buried out of the public treasury,

for they could not endure the stench. But afterward, when they were not able to do this, they threw the bodies from the walls into the trenches.

18. And as Titus went around and saw the trenches filled with the dead, and the thick blood oozing out of the putrid bodies, he groaned aloud, and, raising his hands, called God to witness that this was not his doing.

19. After speaking of some other things, Josephus proceeds as follows: **"I cannot hesitate to declare what my feelings compel me to. I suppose, if the Romans had longer delayed in coming against these guilty wretches, the city would have been swallowed up by a chasm, or overwhelmed with a flood, or struck with such thunderbolts as destroyed Sodom. For it had brought forth a generation of men much more godless than were those that suffered such punishment. By their madness indeed was the whole people brought to destruction."**

20. And in the sixth book he writes as follows: Of those that perished by famine in the city the number was countless, and the miseries they underwent unspeakable. For if so much as the shadow of food appeared in any house, there was war, and the dearest friends engaged in hand-to-hand conflict with one another, and snatched from each other the most wretched supports of life.

21. Nor would they believe that even the dying were without food; but the robbers would search them while they were expiring, lest any one should feign death while concealing food in his bosom. With mouths gaping for want of food, they stumbled and staggered along like mad dogs, and beat the doors as if they were drunk, and in their impotence they would rush into the same houses twice or thrice in one hour.

22. Necessity compelled them to eat anything they could find, and they gathered and devoured things that were not fit even for the filthiest of irrational beasts. Finally

they did not abstain even from their girdles and shoes, and they stripped the hides off their shields and devoured them. Some used even wisps of old hay for food, and others gathered stubble and sold the smallest weight of it for four Attic drachmæ.

23. But why should I speak of the shamelessness which was displayed during the famine toward inanimate things? For I am going to relate a fact such as is recorded neither by Greeks nor Barbarians; horrible to relate, incredible to hear. And indeed I should gladly have omitted this calamity, that I might not seem to posterity to be a teller of fabulous tales, if I had not innumerable witnesses to it in my own age. And besides, I should render my country poor service if I suppressed the account of the sufferings which she endured.

24. There was a certain woman named Mary that dwelt beyond Jordan, whose father was Eleazer, of the village of Bathezor (which signifies the **house of hyssop**).

She was distinguished for her family and her wealth, and had fled with the rest of the multitude to Jerusalem and was shut up there with them during the siege.

25. The tyrants had robbed her of the rest of the property which she had brought with her into the city from Perea. And the remnants of her possessions and whatever food was to be seen the guards rushed in daily and snatched away from her. This made the woman terribly angry, and by her frequent reproaches and imprecations she aroused the anger of the rapacious villains against herself.

26. But no one either through anger or pity would slay her; and she grew weary of finding food for others to eat. The search, too, was already become everywhere difficult, and the famine was piercing her bowels and marrow, and resentment was raging more violently than famine. Taking, therefore, anger and necessity as her counsellors, she proceeded to do a most

unnatural thing.

27. Seizing her child, a boy which was sucking at her breast, she said, Oh, wretched child, in war, in famine, in sedition, for what do I preserve you? Slaves among the Romans we shall be even if we are allowed to live by them. But even slavery is anticipated by the famine, and the rioters are more cruel than both. Come, be food for me, a fury for these rioters, and a bye-word to the world, for this is all that is wanting to complete the calamities of the Jews.

28. And when she had said this she slew her son; and having roasted him, she ate one half herself, and covering up the remainder, she kept it. Very soon the rioters appeared on the scene, and, smelling the nefarious odor, they threatened to slay her immediately unless she should show them what she had prepared. She replied that she had saved an excellent portion for them, and with that she uncovered the remains of the child.

29. They were immediately seized with horror and amazement and stood transfixed at the sight. But she said, This is my own son, and the deed is mine. Eat for I too have eaten. Be not more merciful than a woman, nor more compassionate than a mother. But if you are too pious and shrink from my sacrifice, I have already eaten of it; let the rest also remain for me.

30. At these words the men went out trembling, in this one case being affrighted; yet with difficulty did they yield that food to the mother. Forthwith the whole city was filled with the awful crime, and as all pictured the terrible deed before their own eyes, they trembled as if they had done it themselves.

31. Those that were suffering from the famine now longed for death; and blessed were they that had died before hearing and seeing miseries like these.

32. Such was the reward which the Jews received for their wickedness and impiety, against the Christ of God.

CHAPTER SEVEN

The Predictions of Christ

1. IT IS FITTING TO add to these accounts the true prediction of our Saviour in which he foretold these very events.

2. His words are as follows: **"Woe unto them that are with child, and to them that give suck in those days! But pray that your flight be not in the winter, neither on the Sabbath day. For there shall be great tribulation, such as was not since the beginning of the world to this time,**

no, nor ever shall be."

3. The historian, reckoning the whole number of the slain, says that eleven hundred thousand persons perished by famine and sword, and that the rest of the rioters and robbers, being betrayed by each other after the taking of the city, were slain. But the tallest of the youths and those that were distinguished for beauty were preserved for the triumph. Of the rest of the multitude, those that were over seventeen years of age were sent as prisoners to labor in the works of Egypt, while still more were scattered through the provinces to meet their death in the theaters by the sword and by beasts. Those under seventeen years of age were carried away to be sold as slaves, and of these alone the number reached ninety thousand.

4. These things took place in this manner in the second year of the reign of Vespasian, in accordance with the prophecies of our Lord and Saviour Jesus Christ, who by

divine power saw them beforehand as if they were already present, and wept and mourned according to the statement of the holy evangelists, who give the very words which he uttered, when, as if addressing Jerusalem herself, he said:

5. **"If you had known, even you, in this day, the things which belong unto your peace! But now they are hid from your eyes. For the days shall come upon you, that your enemies shall cast a rampart about you, and compass you round, and keep you in on every side, and shall lay you and your children even with the ground."**

6. And then, as if speaking concerning the people, he says, **"For there shall be great distress in the land, and wrath upon this people. And they shall fall by the edge of the sword, and shall be led away captive into all nations. And Jerusalem shall be trodden down of the Gentiles, until the times of the Gentiles**

be fulfilled." And again: **"When you shall see Jerusalem compassed with armies, then know that the desolation thereof is near.**"

7. If any one compares the words of our Saviour with the other accounts of the historian concerning the whole war, how can one fail to wonder, and to admit that the foreknowledge and the prophecy of our Saviour were truly divine and marvellously strange.

8. Concerning those calamities, then, that befell the whole Jewish nation after the Saviour's passion and after the words which the multitude of the Jews uttered, when they begged the release of the robber and murderer, but besought that the Prince of Life should be taken from their midst, it is not necessary to add anything to the account of the historian.

9. But it may be proper to mention also those events which exhibited the graciousness of that all-good Providence which held back

their destruction full forty years after their crime against Christ – during which time many of the apostles and disciples, and James himself the first bishop there, the one who is called the brother of the Lord, were still alive, and dwelling in Jerusalem itself, remained the surest bulwark of the place. Divine Providence thus still proved itself long-suffering toward them in order to see whether by repentance for what they had done they might obtain pardon and salvation; and in addition to such long-suffering, Providence also furnished wonderful signs of the things which were about to happen to them if they did not repent.

10. Since these matters have been thought worthy of mention by the historian already cited, we cannot do better than to recount them for the benefit of the readers of this work.

CHAPTER EIGHT

The Signs which
preceded the War

1. TAKING, THEN, the work of this author, read what he records in the sixth book of his History. His words are as follows: Thus were the miserable people won over at this time by the impostors and false prophets; but they did not heed nor give credit to the visions and signs that foretold the approaching desolation. On the contrary, as if struck

by lightning, and as if possessing neither eyes nor understanding, they slighted the proclamations of God.

2. At one time a star, in form like a sword, stood over the city, and a comet, which lasted for a whole year; and again before the revolt and before the disturbances that led to the war, when the people were gathered for the feast of unleavened bread, on the eighth of the month Xanthicus, at the ninth hour of the night, so great a light shone about the altar and the temple that it seemed to be bright day; and this continued for half an hour. This seemed to the unskillful a good sign, but was interpreted by the sacred scribes as portending those events which very soon took place.

3. And at the same feast a cow, led by the high priest to be sacrificed, brought forth a lamb in the midst of the temple.

4. And the eastern gate of the inner temple, which was of bronze and very massive, and which at evening was closed with difficulty

by twenty men, and rested upon iron-bound beams, and had bars sunk deep in the ground, was seen at the sixth hour of the night to open of itself.

5. And not many days after the feast, on the twenty-first of the month Artemisium, a certain marvelous vision was seen which passes belief. The prodigy might seem fabulous were it not related by those who saw it, and were not the calamities which followed deserving of such signs. For before the setting of the sun chariots and armed troops were seen throughout the whole region in mid-air, wheeling through the clouds and encircling the cities.

6. And at the feast which is called Pentecost, when the priests entered the temple at night, as was their custom, to perform the services, they said that at first they perceived a movement and a noise, and afterward a voice as of a great multitude, saying, 'Let us go hence.'

7. But what follows is still more terrible; for a

certain Jesus, the son of Ananias, a common countryman, four years before the war, when the city was particularly prosperous and peaceful, came to the feast, at which it was customary for all to make tents at the temple to the honor of God, and suddenly began to cry out: 'A voice from the east, a voice from the west, a voice from the four winds, a voice against Jerusalem and the temple, a voice against bridegrooms and brides, a voice against all the people.' Day and night he went through all the alleys crying thus.

8. But certain of the more distinguished citizens, vexed at the ominous cry, seized the man and beat him with many stripes. But without uttering a word in his own behalf, or saying anything in particular to those that were present, he continued to cry out in the same words as before.

9. And the rulers, thinking, as was true, that the man was moved by a higher power, brought him before the Roman governor. And then, though he was scourged to the

bone, he neither made supplication nor shed tears, but, changing his voice to the most lamentable tone possible, he answered each stroke with the words, 'Woe, woe unto Jerusalem.'

10. The same historian records another fact still more wonderful than this. He says that a certain oracle was found in their sacred writings which declared that at that time a certain person should go forth from their country to rule the world. He himself understood that this was fulfilled in Vespasian.

11. But Vespasian did not rule the whole world, but only that part of it which was subject to the Romans. With better right could it be applied to Christ; to whom it was said by the Father, **"Ask of me, and I will give you the heathen for your inheritance, and the ends of the earth for your possession."** At that very time, indeed, the voice of his holy apostles **"went throughout all the earth, and their words to the end of the world."**

CHAPTER NINE

Josephus and the Works which he has left

1. AFTER ALL THIS IT is fitting that we should know something in regard to the origin and family of Josephus, who has contributed so much to the history in hand. He himself gives us information on this point in the following words: "**Josephus, the son of Mattathias, a priest of Jerusalem, who himself fought against the Romans in**

the beginning and was compelled to be present at what happened afterward."

2. He was the most noted of all the Jews of that day, not only among his own people, but also among the Romans, so that he was honored by the erection of a statue in Rome, and his works were deemed worthy of a place in the library.

3. He wrote the whole of the **Antiquities of the Jews** in twenty books, and a history of the war with the Romans which took place in his time, in seven books. He himself testifies that the latter work was not only written in Greek, but that it was also translated by himself into his native tongue. He is worthy of credit here because of his truthfulness in other matters.

4. There are extant also two other books of his which are worth reading. They treat of the antiquity of the Jews, and in them he replies to Apion the Grammarian, who had at that time written a treatise against the Jews, and also to others who had attempted

to vilify the hereditary institutions of the Jewish people.

5. In the first of these books he gives the number of the canonical books of the so-called Old Testament. Apparently drawing his information from ancient tradition, he shows what books were accepted without dispute among the Hebrews. His words are as follows.

CHAPTER TEN

The Manner in which Josephus mentions the Divine Books

1. WE HAVE NOT, therefore, a multitude of books disagreeing and conflicting with one another; but we have only twenty-two, which contain the record of all time and are justly held to be divine.

2. Of these, five are by Moses, and contain the laws and the tradition respecting the origin of man, and continue the history down

to his own death. This period embraces nearly three thousand years.

3. From the death of Moses to the death of Artaxerxes, who succeeded Xerxes as king of Persia, the prophets that followed Moses wrote the history of their own times in thirteen books. The other four books contain hymns to God, and precepts for the regulation of the life of men.

4. From the time of Artaxerxes to our own day all the events have been recorded, but the accounts are not worthy of the same confidence that we repose in those which preceded them, because there has not been during this time an exact succession of prophets.

5. How much we are attached to our own writings is shown plainly by our treatment of them. For although so great a period has already passed by, no one has ventured either to add to or to take from them, but it is inbred in all Jews from their very birth to regard them as the teachings of God,

and to abide by them, and, if necessary, cheerfully to die for them.

These remarks of the historian I have thought might advantageously be introduced in this connection.

6. Another work of no little merit has been produced by the same writer, **On the Supremacy of Reason**, which some have called **Maccabaicum**, because it contains an account of the struggles of those Hebrews who contended manfully for the true religion, as is related in the books called Maccabees.

7. And at the end of the twentieth book of his Antiquities Josephus himself intimates that he had purposed to write a work in four books concerning God and his existence, according to the traditional opinions of the Jews, and also concerning the laws, why it is that they permit some things while prohibiting others. And the same writer also mentions in his own works other books written by himself.

8. In addition to these things it is proper

to quote also the words that are found at the close of his Antiquities, in confirmation of the testimony which we have drawn from his accounts. In that place he attacks Justus of Tiberias, who, like himself, had attempted to write a history of contemporary events, on the ground that he had not written truthfully. Having brought many other accusations against the man, he continues in these words:

9. I indeed was not afraid in respect to my writings as you were, but, on the contrary, I presented my books to the emperors themselves when the events were almost under men's eyes. For I was conscious that I had preserved the truth in my account, and hence was not disappointed in my expectation of obtaining their attestation.

10. And I presented my history also to many others, some of whom were present at the war, as, for instance, King Agrippa and some of his relatives.

11. For the Emperor Titus desired so much

that the knowledge of the events should be communicated to men by my history alone, that he endorsed the books with his own hand and commanded that they should be published. And King Agrippa wrote sixty-two epistles testifying to the truthfulness of my account. Of these epistles Josephus subjoins two. But this will suffice in regard to him. Let us now proceed with our history.

CHAPTER ELEVEN

Symeon rules the Church of Jerusalem after James

1. AFTER THE MARTYRDOM OF James and the conquest of Jerusalem which immediately followed, it is said that those of the apostles and disciples of the Lord that were still living came together from all directions with those that were related to the Lord according to the flesh (for the majority of them also were still alive) to take counsel

as to who was worthy to succeed James.

2. They all with one consent pronounced Symeon, the son of Clopas, of whom the Gospel also makes mention; to be worthy of the episcopal throne of that parish. He was a cousin, as they say, of the Saviour. For Hegesippus records that Clopas was a brother of Joseph.

CHAPTER TWELVE
Vespasian commands the Descendants of David to be sought

HE ALSO RELATES THAT Vespasian after the conquest of Jerusalem gave orders that all that belonged to the lineage of David should be sought out, in order that none of the royal race might be left among the Jews; and in consequence of this a most terrible persecution again hung over the Jews.

CHAPTER THIRTEEN

Anencletus, the Second Bishop of Rome

AFTER VESPASIAN HAD REIGNED ten years Titus, his son, succeeded him. In the second year of his reign, Linus, who had been bishop of the church of Rome for twelve years, delivered his office to Anencletus. But Titus was succeeded by his brother Domitian after he had reigned two years and the same number of months.

278

CHAPTER FOURTEEN

Abilius, the Second
Bishop of Alexandria

IN THE FOURTH YEAR of Domitian, Annianus, the first bishop of the parish of Alexandria, died after holding office twenty-two years, and was succeeded by Abilius, the second bishop.

CHAPTER FIFTEEN

Clement, the Third Bishop of Rome

IN THE TWELFTH YEAR of the same reign Clement succeeded Anencletus after the latter had been bishop of the church of Rome for twelve years. The apostle in his Epistle to the Philippians informs us that this Clement was his fellow-worker. His words are as follows: **"With Clement and the rest of my fellow-laborers whose names are in the book of life."**

CHAPTER SIXTEEN

The Epistle of Clement

THERE IS EXTANT AN epistle of this Clement which is acknowledged to be genuine and is of considerable length and of remarkable merit. He wrote it in the name of the church of Rome to the church of Corinth, when a sedition had arisen in the latter church. We know that this epistle also has been publicly used in a great many churches both in former times and in our own. And of the fact that a sedition did take place in the church of Corinth at the time referred to Hegesippus is a trustworthy witness.

CHAPTER SEVENTEEN

The Persecution under Domitian

DOMITIAN, HAVING SHOWN great cruelty toward many, and having unjustly put to death no small number of well-born and notable men at Rome, and having without cause exiled and confiscated the property of a great many other illustrious men, finally became a successor of Nero in his hatred and enmity toward God. He was in fact the second that stirred up a persecution against us, although his father Vespasian had undertaken nothing prejudicial to us.

CHAPTER EIGHTEEN
The Apostle John and the
Apocalypse

1. IT IS SAID THAT in this persecution the apostle and evangelist John, who was still alive, was condemned to dwell on the island of Patmos in consequence of his testimony to the divine word.

2. Irenæus, in the fifth book of his work Against Heresies, where he discusses the number of the name of Antichrist which is

given in the so-called Apocalypse of John, speaks as follows concerning him:

3. **"If it were necessary for his name to be proclaimed openly at the present time, it would have been declared by him who saw the revelation. For it was seen not long ago, but almost in our own generation, at the end of the reign of Domitian."**

4. To such a degree, indeed, did the teaching of our faith flourish at that time that even those writers who were far from our religion did not hesitate to mention in their histories the persecution and the martyrdoms which took place during it.

5. And they, indeed, accurately indicated the time. For they recorded that in the fifteenth year of Domitian Flavia Domitilla, daughter of a sister of Flavius Clement, who at that time was one of the consuls of Rome, was exiled with many others to the island of Pontia in consequence of testimony borne to Christ.

CHAPTER NINETEEN

Domitian commands the Descendants of David to be slain

BUT WHEN THIS SAME Domitian had commanded that the descendants of David should be slain, an ancient tradition says that some of the heretics brought accusation against the descendants of Jude (said to have been a brother of the Saviour according to the flesh), on the ground that they were of the lineage of David and were related to Christ himself. Hegesippus relates these facts in the following words.

CHAPTER TWENTY

The Relatives of our Saviour

1. OF THE FAMILY OF the Lord there were still living the grandchildren of Jude, who is said to have been the Lord's brother according to the flesh.

2. Information was given that they belonged to the family of David, and they were brought to the Emperor Domitian by the Evocatus. For Domitian feared the coming of Christ as Herod also had feared it. And he asked them

if they were descendants of David, and they confessed that they were. Then he asked them how much property they had, or how much money they owned. And both of them answered that they had only nine thousand denarii, half of which belonged to each of them.

4. And this property did not consist of silver, but of a piece of land which contained only thirty-nine acres, and from which they raised their taxes and supported themselves by their own labor.

5. Then they showed their hands, exhibiting the hardness of their bodies and the callousness produced upon their hands by continuous toil as evidence of their own labor.

6. And when they were asked concerning Christ and his kingdom, of what sort it was and where and when it was to appear, they answered that it was not a temporal nor an earthly kingdom, but a heavenly and angelic one, which would appear at the end

of the world, when he should come in glory to judge the quick and the dead, and to give unto every one according to his works.

7. Upon hearing this, Domitian did not pass judgment against them, but, despising them as of no account, he let them go, and by a decree put a stop to the persecution of the Church.

8. But when they were released they ruled the churches because they were witnesses and were also relatives of the Lord. And peace being established, they lived until the time of Trajan. These things are related by Hegesippus.

9. Tertullian also has mentioned Domitian in the following words: **"Domitian also, who possessed a share of Nero's cruelty, attempted once to do the same thing that the latter did. But because he had, I suppose, some intelligence, he very soon ceased, and even recalled those whom he had banished."**

10. But after Domitian had reigned fifteen

years, and Nerva had succeeded to the empire, the Roman Senate, according to the writers that record the history of those days, voted that Domitian's honors should be cancelled, and that those who had been unjustly banished should return to their homes and have their property restored to them.

11. It was at this time that the apostle John returned from his banishment in the island and took up his abode at Ephesus, according to an ancient Christian tradition.

CHAPTER TWENTY ONE

Cerdon becomes the Third Ruler of the Church of Alexandria

1. AFTER NERVA HAD REIGNED a little more than a year he was succeeded by Trajan. It was during the first year of his reign that Abilius, who had ruled the church of Alexandria for thirteen years, was succeeded by Cerdon.

2. He was the third that presided over that church after Annianus, who was the first. At that time Clement still ruled the church of Rome, being also the third that held the episcopate there after Paul and Peter.

3. Linus was the first, and after him came Anencletus.

CHAPTER TWENTY TWO

Ignatius, the Second Bishop of Antioch

AT THIS TIME IGNATIUS was known as the second bishop of Antioch, Evodius having been the first. Symeon likewise was at that time the second ruler of the church of Jerusalem, the brother of our Saviour having been the first.

295

CHAPTER TWENTY THREE

Narrative Concerning John the Apostle

1. AT THAT TIME THE apostle and evangelist John, the one whom Jesus loved, was still living in Asia, and governing the churches of that region, having returned after the death of Domitian from his exile on the island.

2. And that he was still alive at that time may be established by the testimony of

two witnesses. They should be trustworthy who have maintained the orthodoxy of the Church; and such indeed were Irenæus and Clement of Alexandria.

3. The former in the second book of his work Against Heresies, writes as follows: **"And all the elders that associated with John the disciple of the Lord in Asia bear witness that John delivered it to them. For he remained among them until the time of Trajan."**

4. And in the third book of the same work he attests the same thing in the following words: **"But the church in Ephesus also, which was founded by Paul, and where John remained until the time of Trajan, is a faithful witness of the apostolic tradition."**

5. Clement likewise in his book entitled What Rich Man can be saved? indicates the time, and subjoins a narrative which is most attractive to those that enjoy hearing what is beautiful and profitable. Take and

read the account which runs as follows:

6. Listen to a tale, which is not a mere tale, but a narrative concerning John the apostle, which has been handed down and treasured up in memory. For when, after the tyrant's death, he returned from the isle of Patmos to Ephesus, he went away upon their invitation to the neighboring territories of the Gentiles, to appoint bishops in some places, in other places to set in order whole churches, elsewhere to choose to the ministry some one of those that were pointed out by the Spirit.

7. When he had come to one of the cities not far away (the name of which is given by some), and had consoled the brethren in other matters, he finally turned to the bishop that had been appointed, and seeing a youth of powerful physique, of pleasing appearance, and of ardent temperament, he said, 'This one I commit to you in all earnestness in the presence of the Church and with Christ as witness.'

And when the bishop had accepted the charge and had promised all, he repeated the same injunction with an appeal to the same witnesses, and then departed for Ephesus.

8. But the presbyter taking home the youth committed to him, reared, kept, cherished, and finally baptized him. After this he relaxed his stricter care and watchfulness, with the idea that in putting upon him the seal of the Lord he had given him a perfect protection.

9. But some youths of his own age, idle and dissolute, and accustomed to evil practices, corrupted him when he was thus prematurely freed from restraint. At first they enticed him by costly entertainments; then, when they went forth at night for robbery, they took him with them, and finally they demanded that he should unite with them in some greater crime.

10. He gradually became accustomed to such practices, and on account of the positiveness of his character, leaving the

right path, and taking the bit in his teeth like a hard-mouthed and powerful horse, he rushed the more violently down into the depths.

11. And finally despairing of salvation in God, he no longer meditated what was insignificant, but having committed some great crime, since he was now lost once for all, he expected to suffer a like fate with the rest. Taking them, therefore, and forming a band of robbers, he became a bold bandit-chief, the most violent, most bloody, most cruel of them all.

12. Time passed, and some necessity having arisen, they sent for John. But he, when he had set in order the other matters on account of which he had come, said, 'Come, O bishop, restore us the deposit which both I and Christ committed to you, the church, over which you preside, being witness.'

13. But the bishop was at first confounded, thinking that he was falsely charged in

regard to money which he had not received, and he could neither believe the accusation respecting what he had not, nor could he disbelieve John. But when he said, 'I demand the young man and the soul of the brother,' the old man, groaning deeply and at the same time bursting into tears, said, 'He is dead.' 'How and what kind of death?' 'He is dead to God,' he said; 'for he turned wicked and abandoned, and at last a robber. And now, instead of the church, he haunts the mountain with a band like himself.'

14. But the Apostle rent his clothes, and beating his head with great lamentation, he said, 'A fine guard I left for a brother's soul! But let a horse be brought me, and let some one show me the way.' He rode away from the church just as he was, and coming to the place, he was taken prisoner by the robbers' outpost.

15. He, however, neither fled nor made entreaty, but cried out, 'For this did I come; lead me to your captain.'

16. The latter, meanwhile, was waiting, armed as he was. But when he recognized John approaching, he turned in shame to flee.

17. But John, forgetting his age, pursued him with all his might, crying out, 'Why, my son, do you flee from me, your own father, unarmed, aged? Pity me, my son; fear not; you have still hope of life. I will give account to Christ for you. If need be, I will willingly endure your death as the Lord suffered death for us. For you will I give up my life. Stand, believe; Christ has sent me.'

18. And he, when he heard, first stopped and looked down; then he threw away his arms, and then trembled and wept bitterly. And when the old man approached, he embraced him, making confession with lamentations as he was able, baptizing himself a second time with tears, and concealing only his right hand.

19. But John, pledging himself, and assuring him on oath that he would find forgiveness

with the Saviour, besought him, fell upon his knees, kissed his right hand itself as if now purified by repentance, and led him back to the church. And making intercession for him with copious prayers, and struggling together with him in continual fastings, and subduing his mind by various utterances, he did not depart, as they say, until he had restored him to the church, furnishing a great example of true repentance and a great proof of regeneration, a trophy of a visible resurrection.

CHAPTER TWENTY FOUR

The Order of the Gospels

1. THIS EXTRACT FROM CLEMENT I have inserted here for the sake of the history and for the benefit of my readers. Let us now point out the undisputed writings of this apostle.

2. And in the first place his Gospel, which is known to all the churches under heaven, must be acknowledged as genuine. That it has with good reason been put by the

ancients in the fourth place, after the other three Gospels, may be made evident in the following way.

3. Those great and truly divine men, I mean the apostles of Christ, were purified in their life, and were adorned with every virtue of the soul, but were uncultivated in speech. They were confident indeed in their trust in the divine and wonder-working power which was granted unto them by the Saviour, but they did not know how, nor did they attempt to proclaim the doctrines of their teacher in studied and artistic language, but employing only the demonstration of the divine Spirit, which worked with them, and the wonder-working power of Christ, which was displayed through them, they published the knowledge of the kingdom of heaven throughout the whole world, paying little attention to the composition of written works.

4. And this they did because they were assisted in their ministry by one greater than

man. Paul, for instance, who surpassed them all in vigor of expression and in richness of thought, committed to writing no more than the briefest epistles, although he had innumerable mysterious matters to communicate, for he had attained even unto the sights of the third heaven, had been carried to the very paradise of God, and had been deemed worthy to hear unspeakable utterances there.

5. And the rest of the followers of our Saviour, the twelve apostles, the seventy disciples, and countless others besides, were not ignorant of these things. Nevertheless, of all the disciples of the Lord, only Matthew and John have left us written memorials, and they, tradition says, were led to write only under the pressure of necessity.

6. For Matthew, who had at first preached to the Hebrews, when he was about to go to other peoples, committed his Gospel to writing in his native tongue, and thus compensated those whom he was obliged

to leave for the loss of his presence.

7. And when Mark and Luke had already published their Gospels, they say that John, who had employed all his time in proclaiming the Gospel orally, finally proceeded to write for the following reason. The three Gospels already mentioned having come into the hands of all and into his own too, they say that he accepted them and bore witness to their truthfulness; but that there was lacking in them an account of the deeds done by Christ at the beginning of his ministry.

8. And this indeed is true. For it is evident that the three evangelists recorded only the deeds done by the Saviour for one year after the imprisonment of John the Baptist, and indicated this in the beginning of their account.

9. For Matthew, after the forty days' fast and the temptation which followed it, indicates the chronology of his work when he says: **"Now when he heard that John was delivered up he withdrew from Judea**

into Galilee." Matthew 4:12

10. Mark likewise says: "**Now after that John was delivered up Jesus came into Galilee.**" Mark 1:14 And Luke, before commencing his account of the deeds of Jesus, similarly marks the time, when he says that Herod, "**adding to all the evil deeds which he had done, shut up John in prison.**" Luke 3:20

11. They say, therefore, that the apostle John, being asked to do it for this reason, gave in his Gospel an account of the period which had been omitted by the earlier evangelists, and of the deeds done by the Saviour during that period; that is, of those which were done before the imprisonment of the Baptist. And this is indicated by him, they say, in the following words: "**This beginning of miracles did Jesus**"; and again when he refers to the Baptist, in the midst of the deeds of Jesus, as still baptizing in Ænon near Salim; John 3:23 where he states the matter clearly in the words: "**For John was**

not yet cast into prison."

12. John accordingly, in his Gospel, records the deeds of Christ which were performed before the Baptist was cast into prison, but the other three evangelists mention the events which happened after that time.

13. One who understands this can no longer think that the Gospels are at variance with one another, inasmuch as the Gospel according to John contains the first acts of Christ, while the others give an account of the latter part of his life. And the genealogy of our Saviour according to the flesh John quite naturally omitted, because it had been already given by Matthew and Luke, and began with the doctrine of his divinity, which had, as it were, been reserved for him, as their superior, by the divine Spirit.

14. These things may suffice, which we have said concerning the Gospel of John. The cause which led to the composition of the Gospel of Mark has been already stated by us.

15. But as for Luke, in the beginning of his Gospel, he states himself the reasons which led him to write it. He states that since many others had more rashly undertaken to compose a narrative of the events of which he had acquired perfect knowledge, he himself, feeling the necessity of freeing us from their uncertain opinions, delivered in his own Gospel an accurate account of those events in regard to which he had learned the full truth, being aided by his intimacy and his stay with Paul and by his acquaintance with the rest of the apostles.

16. So much for our own account of these things. But in a more fitting place we shall attempt to show by quotations from the ancients, what others have said concerning them.

17. But of the writings of John, not only his Gospel, but also the former of his epistles, has been accepted without dispute both now and in ancient times. But the other two are disputed.

18. In regard to the Apocalypse, the opinions of most men are still divided. But at the proper time this question likewise shall be decided from the testimony of the ancients.

CHAPTER TWENTY FIVE

The Divine Scriptures that are accepted and those that are not

1. SINCE WE ARE DEALING with this subject it is proper to sum up the writings of the New Testament which have been already mentioned. First then must be put the holy quaternion of the Gospels; following them the Acts of the Apostles.

2. After this must be reckoned the epistles of Paul; next in order the extant former epistle of John, and likewise the epistle of Peter, must be maintained. After them is to be placed, if it really seem proper, the Apocalypse of John, concerning which we shall give the different opinions at the proper time. These then belong among the accepted writings.

3. Among the disputed writings, which are nevertheless recognized by many, are extant the so-called epistle of James and that of Jude, also the second epistle of Peter, and those that are called the second and third of John, whether they belong to the evangelist or to another person of the same name.

4. Among the rejected writings must be reckoned also the Acts of Paul, and the so-called Shepherd, and the Apocalypse of Peter, and in addition to these the extant epistle of Barnabas, and the so-called Teachings of the Apostles; and besides, as

I said, the Apocalypse of John, if it seem proper, which some, as I said, reject, but which others class with the accepted books.

5. And among these some have placed also the Gospel according to the Hebrews, with which those of the Hebrews that have accepted Christ are especially delighted. And all these may be reckoned among the disputed books.

6. But we have nevertheless felt compelled to give a catalogue of these also, distinguishing those works which according to ecclesiastical tradition are true and genuine and commonly accepted, from those others which, although not canonical but disputed, are yet at the same time known to most ecclesiastical writers – we have felt compelled to give this catalogue in order that we might be able to know both these works and those that are cited by the heretics under the name of the apostles, including, for instance, such books as the Gospels of Peter, of Thomas,

of Matthias, or of any others besides them, and the Acts of Andrew and John and the other apostles, which no one belonging to the succession of ecclesiastical writers has deemed worthy of mention in his writings.

7. And further, the character of the style is at variance with apostolic usage, and both the thoughts and the purpose of the things that are related in them are so completely out of accord with true orthodoxy that they clearly show themselves to be the fictions of heretics. Wherefore they are not to be placed even among the rejected writings, but are all of them to be cast aside as absurd and impious.

Let us now proceed with our history.

CHAPTER TWENTY SIX
Menander the Sorcerer

1. MENANDER, WHO SUCCEEDED Simon Magus, showed himself in his conduct another instrument of diabolical power, not inferior to the former. He also was a Samaritan and carried his sorceries to no less an extent than his teacher had done, and at the same time reveled in still more marvelous tales than he.

2. For he said that he was himself the

Saviour, who had been sent down from invisible æons for the salvation of men; and he taught that no one could gain the mastery over the world-creating angels themselves unless he had first gone through the magical discipline imparted by him and had received baptism from him. Those who were deemed worthy of this would partake even in the present life of perpetual immortality, and would never die, but would remain here forever, and without growing old become immortal. These facts can be easily learned from the works of Irenæus.

3. And Justin, in the passage in which he mentions Simon, gives an account of this man also, in the following words: **"And we know that a certain Menander, who was also a Samaritan, from the village of Capparattea, was a disciple of Simon, and that he also, being driven by the demons, came to Antioch and deceived many by his magical art. And he persuaded his followers that they should not die. And**

there are still some of them that assert this.''

4. And it was indeed an artifice of the devil to endeavor, by means of such sorcerers, who assumed the name of Christians, to defame the great mystery of godliness by magic art, and through them to make ridiculous the doctrines of the Church concerning the immortality of the soul and the resurrection of the dead. But they that have chosen these men as their saviours have fallen away from the true hope.

CHAPTER TWENTY SEVEN

The Heresy of the Ebionites

1. THE EVIL DEMON, however, being unable to tear certain others from their allegiance to the Christ of God, yet found them susceptible in a different direction, and so brought them over to his own purposes. The ancients quite properly called these men Ebionites, because they held poor and mean opinions concerning Christ.

2. For they considered him a plain and

common man, who was justified only because of his superior virtue, and who was the fruit of the intercourse of a man with Mary. In their opinion the observance of the ceremonial law was altogether necessary, on the ground that they could not be saved by faith in Christ alone and by a corresponding life.

3. There were others, however, besides them, that were of the same name, but avoided the strange and absurd beliefs of the former, and did not deny that the Lord was born of a virgin and of the Holy Spirit. But nevertheless, inasmuch as they also refused to acknowledge that he pre-existed, being God, Word, and Wisdom, they turned aside into the impiety of the former, especially when they, like them, endeavored to observe strictly the bodily worship of the law.

4. These men, moreover, thought that it was necessary to reject all the epistles of the apostle, whom they called an apostate

from the law; and they used only the so-called Gospel according to the Hebrews and made small account of the rest.

5. The Sabbath and the rest of the discipline of the Jews they observed just like them, but at the same time, like us, they celebrated the Lord's days as a memorial of the resurrection of the Saviour.

6. Wherefore, in consequence of such a course they received the name of Ebionites, which signified the poverty of their understanding. For this is the name by which a poor man is called among the Hebrews.

CHAPTER TWENTY EIGHT

Cerinthus the Heresiarch

1. WE HAVE UNDERSTOOD THAT at this time Cerinthus, the author of another heresy, made his appearance. Caius, whose words we quoted above, in the Disputation which is ascribed to him, writes as follows concerning this man:

2. **"But Cerinthus also, by means of revelations which he pretends were written by a great apostle, brings before**

us marvelous things which he falsely claims were shown him by angels; and he says that after the resurrection the kingdom of Christ will be set up on earth, and that the flesh dwelling in Jerusalem will again be subject to desires and pleasures. And being an enemy of the Scriptures of God, he asserts, with the purpose of deceiving men, that there is to be a period of a thousand years for marriage festivals."

3. And Dionysius, who was bishop of the parish of Alexandria in our day, in the second book of his work **On the Promises**, where he says some things concerning the Apocalypse of John which he draws from tradition, mentions this same man in the following words:

4. But (they say that) Cerinthus, who founded the sect which was called, after him, the Cerinthian, desiring reputable authority for his fiction, prefixed the name. For the doctrine which he taught was this:

that the kingdom of Christ will be an earthly one.

5. And as he was himself devoted to the pleasures of the body and altogether sensual in his nature, he dreamed that that kingdom would consist in those things which he desired, namely, in the delights of the belly and of sexual passion, that is to say, in eating and drinking and marrying, and in festivals and sacrifices and the slaying of victims, under the guise of which he thought he could indulge his appetites with a better grace.

6. These are the words of Dionysius. But Irenæus, in the first book of his work Against Heresies, gives some more abominable false doctrines of the same man, and in the third book relates a story which deserves to be recorded. He says, on the authority of Polycarp, that the apostle John once entered a bath to bathe; but, learning that Cerinthus was within, he sprang from the place and rushed out of the door, for he could not bear

to remain under the same roof with him. And he advised those that were with him to do the same, saying, **"Let us flee, lest the bath fall; for Cerinthus, the enemy of the truth, is within."**

CHAPTER TWENTY NINE

Nicolaus and the Sect named after him

1. AT THIS TIME THE so-called sect of the Nicolaitans made its appearance and lasted for a very short time. Mention is made of it in the Apocalypse of John. They boasted that the author of their sect was Nicolaus, one of the deacons who, with Stephen, were appointed by the apostles for the purpose of ministering to the poor. Clement of

Alexandria, in the third book of his Stromata, relates the following things concerning him.

2. They say that he had a beautiful wife, and after the ascension of the Saviour, being accused by the apostles of jealousy, he led her into their midst and gave permission to any one that wished to marry her. For they say that this was in accord with that saying of his, that one ought to abuse the flesh. And those that have followed his heresy, imitating blindly and foolishly that which was done and said, commit fornication without shame.

3. But I understand that Nicolaus had to do with no other woman than her to whom he was married, and that, so far as his children are concerned, his daughters continued in a state of virginity until old age, and his son remained uncorrupt. If this is so, when he brought his wife, whom he jealously loved, into the midst of the apostles, he was evidently renouncing his passion; and when he used the expression,

'to abuse the flesh,' he was inculcating self-control in the face of those pleasures that are eagerly pursued. For I suppose that, in accordance with the command of the Saviour, he did not wish to serve two masters, pleasure and the Lord.

4. But they say that Matthias also taught in the same manner that we ought to fight against and abuse the flesh, and not give way to it for the sake of pleasure, but strengthen the soul by faith and knowledge. So much concerning those who then attempted to pervert the truth, but in less time than it has taken to tell it became entirely extinct.

CHAPTER THIRTY

The Apostles that were Married

1. CLEMENT, INDEED, whose words we have just quoted, after the above-mentioned facts gives a statement, on account of those who rejected marriage, of the apostles that had wives. **"Or will they,"** says he, **"reject even the apostles? For Peter and Philip begot children; and Philip also gave his daughters in marriage. And Paul does not hesitate, in one of his epistles, to**

greet his wife, whom he did not take about with him, that he might not be inconvenienced in his ministry."

2. And since we have mentioned this subject it is not improper to subjoin another account which is given by the same author and which is worth reading. In the seventh book of his Stromata he writes as follows: "**They say, accordingly, that when the blessed Peter saw his own wife led out to die, he rejoiced because of her summons and her return home, and called to her very encouragingly and comfortingly, addressing her by name, and saying, 'Remember the Lord.' Such was the marriage of the blessed, and their perfect disposition toward those dearest to them.**" This account being in keeping with the subject in hand, I have related here in its proper place.

CHAPTER THIRTY ONE

The Death of John and Philip

1. THE TIME AND THE manner of the death of Paul and Peter as well as their burial places, have been already shown by us.

2. The time of John's death has also been given in a general way, but his burial place is indicated by an epistle of Polycrates (who was bishop of the parish of Ephesus), addressed to Victor, bishop of Rome. In this epistle he mentions him together with

the apostle Philip and his daughters in the following words:

3. **"For in Asia also great lights have fallen asleep, which shall rise again on the last day, at the coming of the Lord, when he shall come with glory from heaven and shall seek out all the saints. Among these are Philip, one of the twelve apostles, who sleeps in Hierapolis, and his two aged virgin daughters, and another daughter who lived in the Holy Spirit and now rests at Ephesus; and moreover John, who was both a witness and a teacher, who reclined upon the bosom of the Lord, and being a priest wore the sacerdotal plate. He also sleeps at Ephesus."**

4. So much concerning their death. And in the Dialogue of Caius which we mentioned a little above, Proclus, against whom he directed his disputation, in agreement with what has been quoted, speaks thus concerning the death of Philip and his daughters: **"After**

him there were four prophetesses, the daughters of Philip, at Hierapolis in Asia. Their tomb is there and the tomb of their father." Such is his statement.

5. But Luke, in the Acts of the Apostles, mentions the daughters of Philip who were at that time at Cæsarea in Judea with their father, and were honored with the gift of prophecy. His words are as follows: **"We came unto Cæsarea; and entering into the house of Philip the evangelist, who was one of the seven, we abode with him. Now this man had four daughters, virgins, which did prophesy."**

6. We have thus set forth in these pages what has come to our knowledge concerning the apostles themselves and the apostolic age, and concerning the sacred writings which they have left us, as well as concerning those which are disputed, but nevertheless have been publicly used by many in a great number of churches, and moreover, concerning those that are altogether rejected and are

out of harmony with apostolic orthodoxy. Having done this, let us now proceed with our history.

CHAPTER THIRTY TWO

Symeon, Bishop of Jerusalem, suffers Martyrdom

1. IT IS REPORTED THAT after the age of Nero and Domitian, under the emperor whose times we are now recording, a persecution was stirred up against us in certain cities in consequence of a popular uprising. In this persecution we have understood that Symeon, the son of Clopas, who, as we have shown, was the second bishop of the

church of Jerusalem, suffered martyrdom.

2. Hegesippus, whose words we have already quoted in various places, is a witness to this fact also. Speaking of certain heretics he adds that Symeon was accused by them at this time; and since it was clear that he was a Christian, he was tortured in various ways for many days, and astonished even the judge himself and his attendants in the highest degree, and finally he suffered a death similar to that of our Lord.

3. But there is nothing like hearing the historian himself, who writes as follows: **"Certain of these heretics brought accusation against Symeon, the son of Clopas, on the ground that he was a descendant of David and a Christian; and thus he suffered martyrdom, at the age of one hundred and twenty years, while Trajan was emperor and Atticus governor."**

4. And the same writer says that his accusers also, when search was made for

the descendants of David, were arrested as belonging to that family. And it might be reasonably assumed that Symeon was one of those that saw and heard the Lord, judging from the length of his life, and from the fact that the Gospel makes mention of Mary, the wife of Clopas, who was the father of Symeon, as has been already shown.

5. The same historian says that there were also others, descended from one of the so-called brothers of the Saviour, whose name was Judas, who, after they had borne testimony before Domitian, as has been already recorded, in behalf of faith in Christ, lived until the same reign.

6. He writes as follows: **"They came, therefore, and took the lead of every church as witnesses and as relatives of the Lord. And profound peace being established in every church, they remained until the reign of the Emperor Trajan, and until the above-mentioned Symeon, son of Clopas, an uncle of**

the Lord, was informed against by the heretics, and was himself in like manner accused for the same cause before the governor Atticus. And after being tortured for many days he suffered martyrdom, and all, including even the proconsul, marveled that, at the age of one hundred and twenty years, he could endure so much. And orders were given that he should be crucified."

7. In addition to these things the same man, while recounting the events of that period, records that the Church up to that time had remained a pure and uncorrupted virgin, since, if there were any that attempted to corrupt the sound norm of the preaching of salvation, they lay until then concealed in obscure darkness.

8. But when the sacred college of apostles had suffered death in various forms, and the generation of those that had been deemed worthy to hear the inspired wisdom with their own ears had passed away, then the league

of godless error took its rise as a result of the folly of heretical teachers, who, because none of the apostles was still living, attempted henceforth, with a bold face, to proclaim, in opposition to the preaching of the truth, the 'knowledge which is falsely so-called.'

CHAPTER THIRTY THREE

Trajan forbids the Christians to be sought after

1. SO GREAT A PERSECUTION was at that time opened against us in many places that Plinius Secundus, one of the most noted of governors, being disturbed by the great number of martyrs, communicated with the emperor concerning the multitude of those that were put to death for their faith. At the same time, he informed him in his

communication that he had not heard of their doing anything profane or contrary to the laws – except that they arose at dawn and sang hymns to Christ as a God; but that they renounced adultery and murder and like criminal offenses, and did all things in accordance with the laws.

2. In reply to this Trajan made the following decree: that the race of Christians should not be sought after, but when found should be punished. On account of this the persecution which had threatened to be a most terrible one was to a certain degree checked, but there were still left plenty of pretexts for those who wished to do us harm. Sometimes the people, sometimes the rulers in various places, would lay plots against us, so that, although no great persecutions took place, local persecutions were nevertheless going on in particular provinces, and many of the faithful endured martyrdom in various forms.

3. We have taken our account from the Latin Apology of Tertullian which we mentioned

above. The translation runs as follows: And indeed we have found that search for us has been forbidden. For when Plinius Secundus, the governor of a province, had condemned certain Christians and deprived them of their dignity, he was confounded by the multitude, and was uncertain what further course to pursue. He therefore communicated with Trajan the emperor, informing him that, aside from their unwillingness to sacrifice, he had found no impiety in them.

4. And he reported this also, that the Christians arose early in the morning and sang hymns unto Christ as a God, and for the purpose of preserving their discipline forbade murder, adultery, avarice, robbery, and the like. In reply to this Trajan wrote that the race of Christians should not be sought after, but when found should be punished. Such were the events which took place at that time.

CHAPTER THIRTY FOUR

Evarestus, the Fourth Bishop of the Church of Rome

1. IN THE THIRD YEAR of the reign of the emperor mentioned above, Clement committed the episcopal government of the church of Rome to Evarestus, and departed this life after he had superintended the teaching of the divine word nine years in all.

CHAPTER THIRTY FIVE

Justus, the Third
Bishop of Jerusalem

1. BUT WHEN SYMEON ALSO had died in the manner described, a certain Jew by the name of Justus succeeded to the episcopal throne in Jerusalem. He was one of the many thousands of the circumcision who at that time believed in Christ.

CHAPTER THIRTY SIX

Ignatius and His Epistles

1. AT THAT TIME POLYCARP, a disciple of the apostles, was a man of eminence in Asia, having been entrusted with the episcopate of the church of Smyrna by those who had seen and heard the Lord.

2. And at the same time Papias, bishop of the parish of Hierapolis, became well known, as did also Ignatius, who was chosen bishop of Antioch, second in succession to

Peter, and whose fame is still celebrated by a great many.

3. Report says that he was sent from Syria to Rome, and became food for wild beasts on account of his testimony to Christ.

4. And as he made the journey through Asia under the strictest military surveillance, he fortified the parishes in the various cities where he stopped by oral homilies and exhortations, and warned them above all to be especially on their guard against the heresies that were then beginning to prevail, and exhorted them to hold fast to the tradition of the apostles. Moreover, he thought it necessary to attest that tradition in writing, and to give it a fixed form for the sake of greater security.

5. So when he came to Smyrna, where Polycarp was, he wrote an epistle to the church of Ephesus, in which he mentions Onesimus, its pastor; and another to the church of Magnesia, situated upon the Mæander, in which he makes mention again

of a bishop Damas; and finally one to the church of Tralles, whose bishop, he states, was at that time Polybius.

6. In addition to these he wrote also to the church of Rome, entreating them not to secure his release from martyrdom, and thus rob him of his earnest hope. In confirmation of what has been said it is proper to quote briefly from this epistle.

7. He writes as follows: From Syria even unto Rome I fight with wild beasts, by land and by sea, by night and by day, being bound amidst ten leopards that is, a company of soldiers who only become worse when they are well treated. In the midst of their wrongdoings, however, I am more fully learning discipleship, but I am not thereby justified.

8. May I have joy of the beasts that are prepared for me; and I pray that I may find them ready; I will even coax them to devour me quickly that they may not treat me as they have some whom they have

refused to touch through fear. And if they are unwilling, I will compel them. Forgive me.

9. I know what is expedient for me. Now do I begin to be a disciple. May nothing of things visible and things invisible envy me; that I may attain unto Jesus Christ. Let fire and cross and attacks of wild beasts, let wrenching of bones, cutting of limbs, crushing of the whole body, tortures of the devil – let all these come upon me if only I may attain unto Jesus Christ.

10. These things he wrote from the above-mentioned city to the churches referred to. And when he had left Smyrna he wrote again from Troas to the Philadelphians and to the church of Smyrna; and particularly to Polycarp, who presided over the latter church. And since he knew him well as an apostolic man, he commended to him, like a true and good shepherd, the flock at Antioch, and besought him to care diligently for it.

11. And the same man, writing to the Smyrnæans, used the following words concerning Christ, taken I know not whence: **"But I know and believe that he was in the flesh after the resurrection. And when he came to Peter and his companions he said to them, Take, handle me, and see that I am not an incorporeal spirit. And immediately they touched him and believed."**

12. Irenæus also knew of his martyrdom and mentions his epistles in the following words: **"As one of our people said, when he was condemned to the beasts on account of his testimony unto God, I am God's wheat, and by the teeth of wild beasts am I ground, that I may be found pure bread."**

13. Polycarp also mentions these letters in the epistle to the Philippians which is ascribed to him. His words are as follows: **"I exhort all of you, therefore, to be obedient and to practice all patience such as you**

saw with your own eyes not only in the blessed Ignatius and Rufus and Zosimus, but also in others from among yourselves as well as in Paul himself and the rest of the apostles; being persuaded that all these ran not in vain, but in faith and righteousness, and that they are gone to their rightful place beside the Lord, with whom also they suffered. For they loved not the present world, but him that died for our sakes and was raised by God for us."

14. And afterwards he adds: You have written to me, both you and Ignatius, that if any one go to Syria he may carry with him the letters from you. And this I will do if I have a suitable opportunity, either I myself or one whom I send to be an ambassador for you also.

15. The epistles of Ignatius which were sent to us by him and the others which we had with us we sent to you as you gave charge. They are appended to this epistle, and from them

you will be able to derive great advantage. For they comprise faith and patience, and every kind of edification that pertains to our Lord. So much concerning Ignatius. But he was succeeded by Heros in the episcopate of the church of Antioch.

CHAPTER THIRTY SEVEN

The Evangelists that were still Eminent at that Time

1. AMONG THOSE THAT WERE celebrated at that time was Quadratus, who, report says, was renowned along with the daughters of Philip for his prophetical gifts. And there were many others besides these who were known in those days, and who occupied the first place among the successors of the apostles. And they

also, being illustrious disciples of such great men, built up the foundations of the churches which had been laid by the apostles in every place, and preached the Gospel more and more widely and scattered the saving seeds of the kingdom of heaven far and near throughout the whole world.

2. For indeed most of the disciples of that time, animated by the divine word with a more ardent love for philosophy, had already fulfilled the command of the Saviour, and had distributed their goods to the needy. Then starting out upon long journeys they performed the office of evangelists, being filled with the desire to preach Christ to those who had not yet heard the word of faith, and to deliver to them the divine Gospels.

3. And when they had only laid the foundations of the faith in foreign places, they appointed others as pastors, and entrusted them with the nurture of those

that had recently been brought in, while they themselves went on again to other countries and nations, with the grace and the co-operation of God. For a great many wonderful works were done through them by the power of the divine Spirit, so that at the first hearing whole multitudes of men eagerly embraced the religion of the Creator of the universe.

4. But since it is impossible for us to enumerate the names of all that became shepherds or evangelists in the churches throughout the world in the age immediately succeeding the apostles, we have recorded, as was fitting, the names of those only who have transmitted the apostolic doctrine to us in writings still extant.

CHAPTER THIRTY EIGHT

The Epistle of Clement and the Writings falsely ascribed to him

1. THUS IGNATIUS HAS DONE in the epistles which we have mentioned, and Clement in his epistle which is accepted by all, and which he wrote in the name of the church of Rome to the church of Corinth. In this epistle he gives many thoughts drawn

from the Epistle to the Hebrews, and also quotes verbally some of its expressions, thus showing most plainly that it is not a recent production.

2. Wherefore it has seemed reasonable to reckon it with the other writings of the apostle. For as Paul had written to the Hebrews in his native tongue, some say that the evangelist Luke, others that this Clement himself, translated the epistle.

3. The latter seems more probable, because the epistle of Clement and that to the Hebrews have a similar character in regard to style, and still further because the thoughts contained in the two works are not very different.

4. But it must be observed also that there is said to be a second epistle of Clement. But we do not know that this is recognized like the former, for we do not find that the ancients have made any use of it.

5. And certain men have lately brought forward other wordy and lengthy writings

under his name, containing dialogues of Peter and Apion. But no mention has been made of these by the ancients; for they do not even preserve the pure stamp of apostolic orthodoxy. The acknowledged writing of Clement is well known. We have spoken also of the works of Ignatius and Polycarp.

CHAPTER THIRTY NINE
The Writings of Papias

1. THERE ARE EXTANT FIVE books of Papias, which bear the title Expositions of Oracles of the Lord. Irenæus makes mention of these as the only works written by him, in the following words: **"These things are attested by Papias, an ancient man who was a hearer of John and a companion of Polycarp, in his fourth book. For five books have been written by him."** These

are the words of Irenæus.

2. But Papias himself in the preface to his discourses by no means declares that he was himself a hearer and eye-witness of the holy apostles, but he shows by the words which he uses that he received the doctrines of the faith from those who were their friends.

3. He says: But I shall not hesitate also to put down for you along with my interpretations whatsoever things I have at any time learned carefully from the elders and carefully remembered, guaranteeing their truth. For I did not, like the multitude, take pleasure in those that speak much, but in those that teach the truth; not in those that relate strange commandments, but in those that deliver the commandments given by the Lord to faith, and springing from the truth itself.

4. If, then, any one came, who had been a follower of the elders, I questioned him in regard to the words of the elders – what

Andrew or what Peter said, or what was said by Philip, or by Thomas, or by James, or by John, or by Matthew, or by any other of the disciples of the Lord, and what things Aristion and the presbyter John, the disciples of the Lord, say. For I did not think that what was to be gotten from the books would profit me as much as what came from the living and abiding voice.

5. It is worth while observing here that the name John is twice enumerated by him. The first one he mentions in connection with Peter and James and Matthew and the rest of the apostles, clearly meaning the evangelist; but the other John he mentions after an interval, and places him among others outside of the number of the apostles, putting Aristion before him, and he distinctly calls him a presbyter.

6. This shows that the statement of those is true, who say that there were two persons in Asia that bore the same name, and that there were two tombs in Ephesus, each of

which, even to the present day, is called John's. It is important to notice this. For it is probable that it was the second, if one is not willing to admit that it was the first that saw the Revelation, which is ascribed by name to John.

7. And Papias, of whom we are now speaking, confesses that he received the words of the apostles from those that followed them, but says that he was himself a hearer of Aristion and the presbyter John. At least he mentions them frequently by name, and gives their traditions in his writings. These things, we hope, have not been uselessly adduced by us.

8. But it is fitting to subjoin to the words of Papias which have been quoted, other passages from his works in which he relates some other wonderful events which he claims to have received from tradition.

9. That Philip the apostle dwelt at Hierapolis with his daughters has been already stated. But it must be noted here

that Papias, their contemporary, says that he heard a wonderful tale from the daughters of Philip. For he relates that in his time one rose from the dead. And he tells another wonderful story of Justus, surnamed Barsabbas: that he drank a deadly poison, and yet, by the grace of the Lord, suffered no harm.

10. The Book of Acts records that the holy apostles after the ascension of the Saviour, put forward this Justus, together with Matthias, and prayed that one might be chosen in place of the traitor Judas, to fill up their number. The account is as follows: **"And they put forward two, Joseph, called Barsabbas, who was surnamed Justus, and Matthias; and they prayed and said."** Acts 1:23

11. The same writer gives also other accounts which he says came to him through unwritten tradition, certain strange parables and teachings of the Saviour, and some other more mythical things.

12. To these belong his statement that there will be a period of some thousand years after the resurrection of the dead, and that the kingdom of Christ will be set up in material form on this very earth. I suppose he got these ideas through a misunderstanding of the apostolic accounts, not perceiving that the things said by them were spoken mystically in figures.

13. For he appears to have been of very limited understanding, as one can see from his discourses. But it was due to him that so many of the Church Fathers after him adopted a like opinion, urging in their own support the antiquity of the man; as for instance Irenæus and any one else that may have proclaimed similar views.

14. Papias gives also in his own work other accounts of the words of the Lord on the authority of Aristion who was mentioned above, and traditions as handed down by the presbyter John; to which we refer those

who are fond of learning. But now we must add to the words of his which we have already quoted the tradition which he gives in regard to Mark, the author of the Gospel.

15. **"This also the presbyter said: Mark, having become the interpreter of Peter, wrote down accurately, though not in order, whatsoever he remembered of the things said or done by Christ. For he neither heard the Lord nor followed him, but afterward, as I said, he followed Peter, who adapted his teaching to the needs of his hearers, but with no intention of giving a connected account of the Lord's discourses, so that Mark committed no error while he thus wrote some things as he remembered them. For he was careful of one thing, not to omit any of the things which he had heard, and not to state any of them falsely."** These things are related by Papias concerning Mark.

16. But concerning Matthew he writes as follows: **"So then Matthew wrote**

the oracles in the Hebrew language, and every one interpreted them as he was able." And the same writer uses testimonies from the first Epistle of John and from that of Peter likewise. And he relates another story of a woman, who was accused of many sins before the Lord, which is contained in the Gospel according to the Hebrews. These things we have thought it necessary to observe in addition to what has been already stated.

BOOK FOUR

CHAPTER ONE

The Bishops of Rome and of Alexandria during the Reign of Trajan

1. ABOUT THE TWELFTH YEAR of the reign of Trajan the above-mentioned bishop of the parish of Alexandria died, and Primus,

the fourth in succession from the apostles, was chosen to the office.

2. At that time also Alexander, the fifth in the line of succession from Peter and Paul, received the episcopate at Rome, after Evarestus had held the office eight years.

CHAPTER TWO

The Calamities of the Jews during Trajan's Reign

1. THE TEACHING AND THE Church of our Saviour flourished greatly and made progress from day to day; but the calamities of the Jews increased, and they underwent a constant succession of evils. In the eighteenth year of Trajan's reign there was another disturbance of the Jews, through which a great multitude of them perished.

2. For in Alexandria and in the rest of Egypt, and also in Cyrene, as if incited by some terrible and factious spirit, they rushed into seditious measures against their fellow-inhabitants, the Greeks. The insurrection increased greatly, and in the following year, while Lupus was governor of all Egypt, it developed into a war of no mean magnitude.

3. In the first attack it happened that they were victorious over the Greeks, who fled to Alexandria and imprisoned and slew the Jews that were in the city. But the Jews of Cyrene, although deprived of their aid, continued to plunder the land of Egypt and to devastate its districts, under the leadership of Lucuas. Against them the emperor sent Marcius Turbo with a foot and naval force and also with a force of cavalry.

4. He carried on the war against them for a long time and fought many battles, and slew many thousands of Jews, not only of

369

those of Cyrene, but also of those who dwelt in Egypt and had come to the assistance of their king Lucuas.

5. But the emperor, fearing that the Jews in Mesopotamia would also make an attack upon the inhabitants of that country, commanded Lucius Quintus to clear the province of them. And he having marched against them slew a great multitude of those that dwelt there; and in consequence of his success he was made governor of Judea by the emperor. These events are recorded also in these very words by the Greek historians that have written accounts of those times.

CHAPTER THREE

The Apologists that wrote in Defense of the Faith during the Reign of Adrian

1. AFTER TRAJAN HAD REIGNED for nineteen and a half years Ælius Adrian became his successor in the empire. To him Quadratus addressed a discourse containing an apology for our religion, because certain wicked men had attempted

to trouble the Christians. The work is still in the hands of a great many of the brethren, as also in our own, and furnishes clear proofs of the man's understanding and of his apostolic orthodoxy.

2. He himself reveals the early date at which he lived in the following words: **"But the works of our Saviour were always present, for they were genuine:– those that were healed, and those that were raised from the dead, who were seen not only when they were healed and when they were raised, but were also always present; and not merely while the Saviour was on earth, but also after his death, they were alive for quite a while, so that some of them lived even to our day."** Such then was Quadratus.

3. Aristides also, a believer earnestly devoted to our religion, left, like Quadratus, an apology for the faith, addressed to Adrian. His work, too, has been preserved even to the present day by a great many persons.

CHAPTER FOUR

The Bishops of Rome and of Alexandria under the Same Emperor

IN THE THIRD YEAR of the same reign, Alexander, bishop of Rome, died after holding office ten years. His successor was Xystus. About the same time Primus, bishop of Alexandria, died in the twelfth year of his episcopate, and was succeeded by Justus.

CHAPTER FIVE

The Bishops of Jerusalem from the Age of our Saviour to the Period under Consideration

1. THE CHRONOLOGY OF THE bishops of Jerusalem I have nowhere found preserved in writing; for tradition says that they were all short lived.

2. But I have learned this much from writings, that until the siege of the Jews,

374

which took place under Adrian, there were fifteen bishops in succession there, all of whom are said to have been of Hebrew descent, and to have received the knowledge of Christ in purity, so that they were approved by those who were able to judge of such matters, and were deemed worthy of the episcopate. For their whole church consisted then of believing Hebrews who continued from the days of the apostles until the siege which took place at this time; in which siege the Jews, having again rebelled against the Romans, were conquered after severe battles.

3. But since the bishops of the circumcision ceased at this time, it is proper to give here a list of their names from the beginning. The first, then, was James, the so-called brother of the Lord; the second, Symeon; the third, Justus; the fourth, Zacchæus; the fifth, Tobias; the sixth, Benjamin; the seventh, John; the eighth, Matthias; the ninth, Philip; the tenth, Seneca; the eleventh, Justus;

the twelfth, Levi; the thirteenth, Ephres; the fourteenth, Joseph; and finally, the fifteenth, Judas.

4. These are the bishops of Jerusalem that lived between the age of the apostles and the time referred to, all of them belonging to the circumcision.

5. In the twelfth year of the reign of Adrian, Xystus, having completed the tenth year of his episcopate, was succeeded by Telesphorus, the seventh in succession from the apostles. In the meantime, after the lapse of a year and some months, Eumenes, the sixth in order, succeeded to the leadership of the Alexandrian church, his predecessor having held office eleven years.

CHAPTER SIX

The Last Siege of the Jews under Adrian

1. AS THE REBELLION OF the Jews at this time grew much more serious, Rufus, governor of Judea, after an auxiliary force had been sent him by the emperor, using their madness as a pretext, proceeded against them without mercy, and destroyed indiscriminately thousands of men and women and children, and in accordance

with the laws of war reduced their country to a state of complete subjection.

2. The leader of the Jews at this time was a man by the name of Barcocheba (which signifies a star), who possessed the character of a robber and a murderer, but nevertheless, relying upon his name, boasted to them, as if they were slaves, that he possessed wonderful powers; and he pretended that he was a star that had come down to them out of heaven to bring them light in the midst of their misfortunes.

3. The war raged most fiercely in the eighteenth year of Adrian, at the city of Bithara, which was a very secure fortress, situated not far from Jerusalem. When the siege had lasted a long time, and the rebels had been driven to the last extremity by hunger and thirst, and the instigator of the rebellion had suffered his just punishment, the whole nation was prohibited from this time on by a decree, and by the commands of Adrian, from ever going up to the country

about Jerusalem. For the emperor gave orders that they should not even see from a distance the land of their fathers. Such is the account of Aristo of Pella.

4. And thus, when the city had been emptied of the Jewish nation and had suffered the total destruction of its ancient inhabitants, it was colonized by a different race, and the Roman city which subsequently arose changed its name and was called **Ælia**, in honor of the emperor Ælius Adrian. And as the church there was now composed of Gentiles, the first one to assume the government of it after the bishops of the circumcision was Marcus.

CHAPTER SEVEN

The Persons that became at that Time Leaders of Knowledge falsely so-called

1. AS THE CHURCHES THROUGHOUT the world were now shining like the most brilliant stars, and faith in our Saviour and Lord Jesus Christ was flourishing among the whole human race, the demon who hates everything that is good, and

is always hostile to the truth, and most bitterly opposed to the salvation of man, turned all his arts against the Church. In the beginning he armed himself against it with external persecutions.

2. But now, being shut off from the use of such means, he devised all sorts of plans, and employed other methods in his conflict with the Church, using base and deceitful men as instruments for the ruin of souls and as ministers of destruction. Instigated by him, impostors and deceivers, assuming the name of our religion, brought to the depth of ruin such of the believers as they could win over, and at the same time, by means of the deeds which they practiced, turned away from the path which leads to the word of salvation those who were ignorant of the faith.

3. Accordingly there proceeded from that Menander, whom we have already mentioned as the successor of Simon, a certain serpent-like power, double-

tongued and two-headed, which produced the leaders of two different heresies, Saturninus, an Antiochian by birth, and Basilides, an Alexandrian. The former of these established schools of godless heresy in Syria, the latter in Alexandria.

4. Irenæus states that the false teaching of Saturninus agreed in most respects with that of Menander, but that Basilides, under the pretext of unspeakable mysteries, invented monstrous fables, and carried the fictions of his impious heresy quite beyond bounds.

5. But as there were at that time a great many members of the Church who were fighting for the truth and defending apostolic and ecclesiastical doctrine with uncommon eloquence, so there were some also that furnished posterity through their writings with means of defense against the heresies to which we have referred.

6. Of these there has come down to us a most powerful refutation of Basilides by

Agrippa Castor, one of the most renowned writers of that day, which shows the terrible imposture of the man.

7. While exposing his mysteries he says that Basilides wrote twenty-four books upon the Gospel, and that he invented prophets for himself named Barcabbas and Barcoph, and others that had no existence, and that he gave them barbarous names in order to amaze those who marvel at such things; that he taught also that the eating of meat offered to idols and the unguarded renunciation of the faith in times of persecution were matters of indifference; and that he enjoined upon his followers, like Pythagoras, a silence of five years.

8. Other similar things the above-mentioned writer has recorded concerning Basilides, and has ably exposed the error of his heresy.

9. Irenæus also writes that Carpocrates was a contemporary of these men, and that he was the father of another heresy, called the heresy of the Gnostics, who did not wish

to transmit any longer the magic arts of Simon, as that one had done, in secret, but openly. For they boasted – as of something great – of love potions that were carefully prepared by them, and of certain demons that sent them dreams and lent them their protection, and of other similar agencies; and in accordance with these things they taught that it was necessary for those who wished to enter fully into their mysteries, or rather into their abominations, to practice all the worst kinds of wickedness, on the ground that they could escape the cosmic powers, as they called them, in no other way than by discharging their obligations to them all by infamous conduct.

10. Thus it came to pass that the malignant demon, making use of these ministers, on the one hand enslaved those that were so pitiably led astray by them to their own destruction, while on the other hand he furnished to the unbelieving heathen abundant opportunities for slandering the divine word, inasmuch as

the reputation of these men brought infamy upon the whole race of Christians.

11. In this way, therefore, it came to pass that there was spread abroad in regard to us among the unbelievers of that age, the infamous and most absurd suspicion that we practiced unlawful commerce with mothers and sisters, and enjoyed impious feasts.

12. He did not, however, long succeed in these artifices, as the truth established itself and in time shone with great brilliancy.

13. For the machinations of its enemies were refuted by its power and speedily vanished. One new heresy arose after another, and the former ones always passed away, and now at one time, now at another, now in one way, now in other ways, were lost in ideas of various kinds and various forms. But the splendor of the catholic and only true Church, which is always the same, grew in magnitude and power, and reflected its piety and simplicity and freedom, and the modesty and purity

of its inspired life and philosophy to every nation both of Greeks and of Barbarians.

14. At the same time the slanderous accusations which had been brought against the whole Church also vanished, and there remained our teaching alone, which has prevailed over all, and which is acknowledged to be superior to all in dignity and temperance, and in divine and philosophical doctrines. So that none of them now ventures to affix a base calumny upon our faith, or any such slander as our ancient enemies formerly delighted to utter.

15. Nevertheless, in those times the truth again called forth many champions who fought in its defense against the godless heresies, refuting them not only with oral, but also with written arguments.

CHAPTER EIGHT
Ecclesiastical Writers

1. AMONG THESE HEGESIPPUS WAS well known. We have already quoted his words a number of times, relating events which happened in the time of the apostles according to his account.

2. He records in five books the true tradition of apostolic doctrine in a most simple style, and he indicates the time in which he flourished when he writes as

follows concerning those that first set up idols: **"To whom they erected cenotaphs and temples, as is done to the present day. Among whom is also Antinoüs, a slave of the Emperor Adrian, in whose honor are celebrated also the Antinoian games, which were instituted in our day. For he [i.e. Adrian] also founded a city named after Antinoüs, and appointed prophets."**

3. At the same time also Justin, a genuine lover of the true philosophy, was still continuing to busy himself with Greek literature. He indicates this time in the Apology which he addressed to Antonine, where he writes as follows: **"We do not think it out of place to mention here Antinoüs also, who lived in our day, and whom all were driven by fear to worship as a god, although they knew who he was and whence he came."**

4. The same writer, speaking of the Jewish war which took place at that time, adds the following: **"For in the late Jewish war**

Barcocheba, the leader of the Jewish rebellion, commanded that Christians alone should be visited with terrible punishments unless they would deny and blaspheme Jesus Christ."

5. And in the same work he shows that his conversion from Greek philosophy to Christianity was not without reason, but that it was the result of deliberation on his part. His words are as follows: **"For I myself, while I was delighted with the doctrines of Plato, and heard the Christians slandered, and saw that they were afraid neither of death nor of anything else ordinarily looked upon as terrible, concluded that it was impossible that they could be living in wickedness and pleasure. For what pleasure-loving or intemperate man, or what man that counts it good to feast on human flesh, could welcome death that he might be deprived of his enjoyments, and would not rather strive to continue**

permanently his present life, and to escape the notice of the rulers, instead of giving himself up to be put to death?"

6. The same writer, moreover, relates that Adrian having received from Serennius Granianus, a most distinguished governor, a letter in behalf of the Christians, in which he stated that it was not just to slay the Christians without a regular accusation and trial, merely for the sake of gratifying the outcries of the populace, sent a rescript to Minucius Fundanus, proconsul of Asia, commanding him to condemn no one without an indictment and a well-grounded accusation.

7. And he gives a copy of the epistle, preserving the original Latin in which it was written, and prefacing it with the following words: **"Although from the epistle of the greatest and most illustrious Emperor Adrian, your father, we have good ground to demand that you order judgment to be given as we have desired, yet we have asked this not because it was ordered**

by Adrian, but rather because we know that what we ask is just. And we have subjoined the copy of Adrian's epistle that you may know that we are speaking the truth in this matter also. And this is the copy."

8. After these words the author referred to gives the rescript in Latin, which we have translated into Greek as accurately as we could. It reads as follows:

CHAPTER NINE

The Epistle of Adrian, decreeing that we should not be punished without a Trial

1. TO MINUCIUS FUNDANUS. I have received an epistle, written to me by Serennius Granianus, a most illustrious man, whom you have succeeded. It does not seem right to me that the matter should be passed by without examination, lest the

men be harassed and opportunity be given to the informers for practicing villainy.

2. If, therefore, the inhabitants of the province can clearly sustain this petition against the Christians so as to give answer in a court of law, let them pursue this course alone, but let them not have resort to men's petitions and outcries. For it is far more proper, if any one wishes to make an accusation, that you should examine into it.

3. If any one therefore accuses them and shows that they are doing anything contrary to the laws, do you pass judgment according to the heinousness of the crime. But, by Hercules! If any one bring an accusation through mere calumny, decide in regard to his criminality, and see to it that you inflict punishment.

Such are the contents of Adrian's rescript.

CHAPTER TEN

The Bishops of Rome and of Alexandria during the Reign of Antoninus

ADRIAN HAVING DIED AFTER a reign of twenty-one years, was succeeded in the government of the Romans by Antoninus, called the Pious. In the first year of his reign Telesphorus died in the eleventh year of his episcopate, and Hyginus became bishop of

Rome. Irenæus records that Telesphorus' death was made glorious by martyrdom, and in the same connection he states that in the time of the above-mentioned Roman bishop Hyginus, Valentinus, the founder of a sect of his own, and Cerdon, the author of Marcion's error, were both well known at Rome. He writes as follows:

CHAPTER ELEVEN
The Heresiarchs of that Age

1. "FOR VALENTINUS CAME TO Rome under Hyginus, flourished under Pius, and remained until Anicetus. Cerdon also, Marcion's predecessor, entered the Church in the time of Hyginus, the ninth bishop, and made confession, and continued in this way, now teaching in secret, now making confession again, and now denounced for corrupt doctrine

and withdrawing from the assembly of the brethren."

2. These words are found in the third book of the work Against Heresies. And again in the first book he speaks as follows concerning Cerdon: **"A certain Cerdon, who had taken his system from the followers of Simon, and had come to Rome under Hyginus, the ninth in the episcopal succession from the apostles, taught that the God proclaimed by the law and prophets was not the father of our Lord Jesus Christ. For the former was known, but the latter unknown; and the former was just, but the latter good. Marcion of Pontus succeeded Cerdon and developed his doctrine, uttering shameless blasphemies."**

3. The same Irenæus unfolds with the greatest vigor the unfathomable abyss of Valentinus' errors in regard to matter, and reveals his wickedness, secret and hidden like a serpent lurking in its nest.

4. And in addition to these men he says that there was also another that lived in that age, Marcus by name, who was remarkably skilled in magic arts. And he describes also their unholy initiations and their abominable mysteries in the following words:

5. **"For some of them prepare a nuptial couch and perform a mystic rite with certain forms of expression addressed to those who are being initiated, and they say that it is a spiritual marriage which is celebrated by them, after the likeness of the marriages above. But others lead them to water, and while they baptize them they repeat the following words: Into the name of the unknown father of the universe, into truth, the mother of all things, into the one that descended upon Jesus. Others repeat Hebrew names in order the better to confound those who are being initiated."**

6. But Hyginus having died at the close of the fourth year of his episcopate, Pius

succeeded him in the government of the church of Rome. In Alexandria Marcus was appointed pastor, after Eumenes had filled the office thirteen years in all. And Marcus having died after holding office ten years was succeeded by Celadion in the government of the church of Alexandria.

7. And in Rome Pius died in the fifteenth year of his episcopate, and Anicetus assumed the leadership of the Christians there. Hegesippus records that he himself was in Rome at this time, and that he remained there until the episcopate of Eleutherus.

8. But Justin was especially prominent in those days. In the guise of a philosopher he preached the divine word, and contended for the faith in his writings. He wrote also a work against Marcion, in which he states that the latter was alive at the time he wrote.

9. He speaks as follows: **"And there is a certain Marcion of Pontus, who is even now still teaching his followers to think that there is some other God greater than**

the Creator. And by the aid of the demons he has persuaded many of every race of men to utter blasphemy, and to deny that the maker of this universe is the father of Christ, and to confess that some other, greater than he, was the creator. And all who followed them are, as we have said, called Christians, just as the name of philosophy is given to philosophers, although they may have no doctrines in common."

10. To this he adds: **"And we have also written a work against all the heresies that have existed, which we will give you if you wish to read it."**

11. But this same Justin contended most successfully against the Greeks, and addressed discourses containing an apology for our faith to the Emperor Antoninus, called Pius, and to the Roman senate. For he lived at Rome. But who and whence he was he shows in his Apology in the following words.

CHAPTER TWELVE

The Apology of Justin addressed to Antoninus

"TO THE EMPEROR Titus Ælius Adrian Antoninus Pius Cæsar Augustus, and to Verissimus his son, the philosopher, and to Lucius the philosopher, own son of Cæsar and adopted son of Pius, a lover of learning, and to the sacred senate and to the whole Roman people, I, Justin, son of Priscus and grandson

of Bacchius, of Flavia Neapolis in Palestine, Syria, present this address and petition in behalf of those men of every nation who are unjustly hated and persecuted, I myself being one of them." And the same emperor having learned also from other brethren in Asia of the injuries of all kinds which they were suffering from the inhabitants of the province, thought it proper to address the following ordinance to the Common Assembly of Asia.

The Epistle of Antoninus to the Common Assembly of Asia in Regard to our Doctrine

1. THE EMPEROR CÆSAR Marcus Aurelius Antoninus Augustus, Armenicus, Pontifex Maximus, for the fifteenth time Tribune, for the third time Consul, to the Common Assembly of Asia, Greeting.

2. I know that the gods also take care that

such persons do not escape detection. For they would much rather punish those who will not worship them than you would.

3. But you throw them into confusion, and while you accuse them of atheism you only confirm them in the opinion which they hold. It would indeed be more desirable for them, when accused, to appear to die for their God, than to live. Wherefore also they come off victorious when they give up their lives rather than yield obedience to your commands.

4. And in regard to the earthquakes which have been and are still taking place, it is not improper to admonish you who lose heart whenever they occur, and nevertheless are accustomed to compare your conduct with theirs.

5. They indeed become the more confident in God, while you, during the whole time, neglect, in apparent ignorance, the other gods and the worship of the Immortal, and oppress and persecute even unto death the

Christians who worship him.

6. But in regard to these persons, many of the governors of the provinces wrote also to our most divine father, to whom he wrote in reply that they should not trouble these people unless it should appear that they were attempting something affecting the Roman government. And to me also many have sent communications concerning these men, but I have replied to them in the same way that my father did.

7. But if any one still persists in bringing accusations against any of these people as such, the person who is accused shall be acquitted of the charge, even if it appear that he is one of them, but the accuser shall be punished. Published in Ephesus in the Common Assembly of Asia.

8. To these things Melito, bishop of the church of Sardis, and a man well known at that time, is a witness, as is clear from his words in the Apology which he addressed to the Emperor Verus in behalf of our doctrine.

CHAPTER FOURTEEN

The Circumstances related of Polycarp, a Friend of the Apostles

1. AT THIS TIME, while Anicetus was at the head of the church of Rome, Irenæus relates that Polycarp, who was still alive, was at Rome, and that he had a conference with Anicetus on a question concerning the day of the paschal feast.

2. And the same writer gives another account of Polycarp which I feel constrained to add to that which has been already related in regard to him. The account is taken from the third book of Irenæus' work Against Heresies, and is as follows:

3. But Polycarp also was not only instructed by the apostles, and acquainted with many that had seen Christ, but was also appointed by apostles in Asia bishop of the church of Smyrna.

4. We too saw him in our early youth; for he lived a long time, and died, when a very old man, a glorious and most illustrious martyr's death, having always taught the things which he had learned from the apostles, which the Church also hands down, and which alone are true.

5. To these things all the Asiatic churches testify, as do also those who, down to the present time, have succeeded Polycarp, who was a much more trustworthy and certain witness of the truth than Valentinus

and Marcion and the rest of the heretics. He also was in Rome in the time of Anicetus and caused many to turn away from the above-mentioned heretics to the Church of God, proclaiming that he had received from the apostles this one and only system of truth which has been transmitted by the Church.

6. And there are those that heard from him that John, the disciple of the Lord, going to bathe in Ephesus and seeing Cerinthus within, ran out of the bath-house without bathing, crying, 'Let us flee, lest even the bath fall, because Cerinthus, the enemy of the truth, is within.'

7. And Polycarp himself, when Marcion once met him and said, 'Do you know us? replied, 'I know the first born of Satan.' Such caution did the apostles and their disciples exercise that they might not even converse with any of those who perverted the truth; as Paul also said, 'A man that is a heretic, after the first and second admonition, reject; knowing he that is such is subverted, and

sins, being condemned of himself.' Titus 3:10-11

8. There is also a very powerful epistle of Polycarp written to the Philippians, from which those that wish to do so, and that are concerned for their own salvation, may learn the character of his faith and the preaching of the truth. Such is the account of Irenæus.

9. But Polycarp, in his above-mentioned epistle to the Philippians, which is still extant, has made use of certain testimonies drawn from the First Epistle of Peter.

10. And when Antoninus, called Pius, had completed the twenty-second year of his reign, Marcus Aurelius Verus, his son, who was also called Antoninus, succeeded him, together with his brother Lucius.

CHAPTER FIFTEEN

Under Verus, Polycarp with Others suffered Martyrdom at Smyrna

1. AT THIS TIME, when the greatest persecutions were exciting Asia, Polycarp ended his life by martyrdom. But I consider it most important that his death, a written account of which is still extant, should be recorded in this history.

2. There is a letter, written in the name of the church over which he himself presided, to the parishes in Pontus, which relates the events that befell him, in the following words:

3. **"The church of God which dwells in Philomelium, and to all the parishes of the holy Catholic Church in every place; mercy and peace and love from God the Father be multiplied. We write unto you, brethren, an account of what happened to those that suffered martyrdom and to the blessed Polycarp, who put an end to the persecution, having, as it were, sealed it by his martyrdom."**

4. After these words, before giving the account of Polycarp, they record the events which befell the rest of the martyrs, and describe the great firmness which they exhibited in the midst of their pains. For they say that the bystanders were struck with amazement when they saw them lacerated with scourges even to the innermost veins

and arteries, so that the hidden inward parts of the body, both their bowels and their members, were exposed to view; and then laid upon sea-shells and certain pointed spits, and subjected to every species of punishment and of torture, and finally thrown as food to wild beasts.

5. And they record that the most noble Germanicus especially distinguished himself, overcoming by the grace of God the fear of bodily death implanted by nature. When indeed the proconsul wished to persuade him, and urged his youth, and besought him, as he was very young and vigorous, to take compassion on himself, he did not hesitate, but eagerly lured the beast toward himself, all but compelling and irritating him, in order that he might the sooner be freed from their unrighteous and lawless life.

6. After his glorious death the whole multitude, marveling at the bravery of the God-beloved martyr and at the fortitude of

the whole race of Christians, began to cry out suddenly, **"Away with the atheists; let Polycarp be sought."**

7. And when a very great tumult arose in consequence of the cries, a certain Phrygian, Quintus by name, who was newly come from Phrygia, seeing the beasts and the additional tortures, was smitten with cowardice and gave up the attainment of salvation.

8. But the above-mentioned epistle shows that he, too hastily and without proper discretion, had rushed forward with others to the tribunal, but when seized had furnished a clear proof to all, that it is not right for such persons rashly and recklessly to expose themselves to danger. Thus did matters turn out in connection with them.

9. But the most admirable Polycarp, when he first heard of these things, continued undisturbed, preserved a quiet and unshaken mind, and determined to remain in the city. But being persuaded by his

friends who entreated and exhorted him to retire secretly, he went out to a farm not far distant from the city and abode there with a few companions, night and day doing nothing but wrestle with the Lord in prayer, beseeching and imploring, and asking peace for the churches throughout the whole world. For this was always his custom.

10. And three days before his arrest, while he was praying, he saw in a vision at night the pillow under his head suddenly seized by fire and consumed; and upon this awakening he immediately interpreted the vision to those that were present, almost foretelling that which was about to happen, and declaring plainly to those that were with him that it would be necessary for him for Christ's sake to die by fire.

11. Then, as those who were seeking him pushed the search with vigor, they say that he was again constrained by the solicitude and love of the brethren to go to another

farm. Thither his pursuers came after no long time, and seized two of the servants there, and tortured one of them for the purpose of learning from him Polycarp's hiding-place.

12. And coming late in the evening, they found him lying in an upper room, whence he might have gone to another house, but he would not, saying, **"The will of God be done."**

13. And when he learned that they were present, as the account says, he went down and spoke to them with a very cheerful and gentle countenance, so that those who did not already know the man thought that they beheld a miracle when they observed his advanced age and the gravity and firmness of his bearing, and they marveled that so much effort should be made to capture a man like him.

14. But he did not hesitate, but immediately gave orders that a table should be spread for them. Then he invited them to partake of a bounteous meal, and asked of them one

hour that he might pray undisturbed. And when they had given permission, he stood up and prayed, being full of the grace of the Lord, so that those who were present and heard him praying were amazed, and many of them now repented that such a venerable and godly old man was about to be put to death.

15. In addition to these things the narrative concerning him contains the following account: But when at length he had brought his prayer to an end, after remembering all that had ever come into contact with him, small and great, famous and obscure, and the whole Catholic Church throughout the world, the hour of departure having come, they put him upon an ass and brought him to the city, it being a great Sabbath. And he was met by Herod, the captain of police, and by his father Nicetes, who took him into their carriage, and sitting beside him endeavored to persuade him, saying, 'For what harm is there in saying, Lord Cæsar, and sacrificing

and saving your life?' He at first did not answer; but when they persisted, he said, 'I am not going to do what you advise me.'

16. And when they failed to persuade him, they uttered dreadful words, and thrust him down with violence, so that as he descended from the carriage he lacerated his shin. But without turning round, he went on his way promptly and rapidly, as if nothing had happened to him, and was taken to the stadium.

17. But there was such a tumult in the stadium that not many heard a voice from heaven, which came to Polycarp as he was entering the place: 'Be strong, Polycarp, and play the man.' And no one saw the speaker, but many of our people heard the voice.

18. And when he was led forward, there was a great tumult, as they heard that Polycarp was taken. Finally, when he came up, the proconsul asked if he were Polycarp. And when he confessed that he was, he endeavored to persuade him to deny,

saying, 'Have regard for your age,' and other like things, which it is their custom to say: 'Swear by the genius of Cæsar; repent and say, Away with the Atheists.'

19. But Polycarp, looking with dignified countenance upon the whole crowd that was gathered in the stadium, waved his hand to them, and groaned, and raising his eyes toward heaven, said, 'Away with the Atheists.'

20. But when the magistrate pressed him, and said, 'Swear, and I will release you; revile Christ,' Polycarp said, 'Fourscore and six years have I been serving him, and he has done me no wrong; how then can I blaspheme my king who saved me?'

21. But when he again persisted, and said, 'Swear by the genius of Cæsar,' Polycarp replied, 'If you vainly suppose that I will swear by the genius of Cæsar, as you say, feigning to be ignorant who I am, hear plainly: I am a Christian. But if you desire to learn the doctrine of Christianity, assign a

day and hear.'

22. The proconsul said, 'Persuade the people.' But Polycarp said, 'As for you, I thought you worthy of an explanation; for we have been taught to render to princes and authorities ordained by God the honor that is due, so long as it does not injure us; but as for these, I do not esteem them the proper persons to whom to make my defense.'

23. But the proconsul said, 'I have wild beasts; I will throw you to them unless you repent.' But he said, 'Call them; for repentance from better to worse is a change we cannot make. But it is a noble thing to turn from wickedness to righteousness.'

24. But he again said to him, 'If you despise the wild beasts, I will cause you to be consumed by fire, unless you repent.' But Polycarp said, 'You threaten a fire which burns for an hour, and after a little is quenched; for you know not the fire of the future judgment and of the eternal punishment which is reserved for the

impious. But why do you delay? Do what you will.'

25. Saying these and other words besides, he was filled with courage and joy, and his face was suffused with grace, so that not only was he not terrified and dismayed by the words that were spoken to him, but, on the contrary, the proconsul was amazed, and sent his herald to proclaim three times in the midst of the stadium: 'Polycarp has confessed that he is a Christian.'

26. And when this was proclaimed by the herald, the whole multitude, both of Gentiles and of Jews, who dwelt in Smyrna, cried out with ungovernable wrath and with a great shout, 'This is the teacher of Asia, the father of the Christians, the overthrower of our gods, who teaches many not to sacrifice nor to worship.'

27. When they had said this, they cried out and asked the Asiarch Philip to let a lion loose upon Polycarp. But he said that it was not lawful for him, since he had closed the

games. Then they thought fit to cry out with one accord that Polycarp should be burned alive.

28. For it was necessary that the vision should be fulfilled which had been shown him concerning his pillow, when he saw it burning while he was praying, and turned and said prophetically to the faithful that were with him, 'I must needs be burned alive.'

29. These things were done with great speed – more quickly than they were said – the crowds immediately collecting from the workshops and baths timber and fagots, the Jews being especially zealous in the work, as is their wont.

30. But when the pile was ready, taking off all his upper garments, and loosing his girdle, he attempted also to remove his shoes, although he had never before done this, because of the effort which each of the faithful always made to touch his skin first; for he had been treated with all honor on

account of his virtuous life even before his gray hairs came.

31. Forthwith then the materials prepared for the pile were placed about him; and as they were also about to nail him to the stake, he said, 'Leave me thus; for he who has given me strength to endure the fire, will also grant me strength to remain in the fire unmoved without being secured by you with nails.' So they did not nail him, but bound him.

32. And he, with his hands behind him, and bound like a noble ram taken from a great flock, an acceptable burnt-offering unto God omnipotent, said,

33. 'Father of your beloved and blessed Son Jesus Christ, through whom we have received the knowledge of you, the God of angels and of powers and of the whole creation and of the entire race of the righteous who live in your presence, I bless you that you have deemed me worthy of this day and hour, that I might receive a portion in the number of the martyrs, in the cup of

Christ, unto resurrection of eternal life, both of soul and of body, in the immortality of the Holy Spirit.

34. Among these may I be received before you this day, in a rich and acceptable sacrifice, as you, the faithful and true God, have beforehand prepared and revealed, and have fulfilled.

35. Wherefore I praise you also for everything; I bless you, I glorify you, through the eternal high priest, Jesus Christ, your beloved Son, through whom, with him, in the Holy Spirit, be glory unto you, both now and for the ages to come, Amen.'

36. When he had offered up his Amen and had finished his prayer, the firemen lighted the fire and as a great flame blazed out, we, to whom it was given to see, saw a wonder, and we were preserved that we might relate what happened to the others.

37. For the fire presented the appearance of a vault, like the sail of a vessel filled by the wind, and made a wall about the body of the

martyr, and it was in the midst not like flesh burning, but like gold and silver refined in a furnace. For we perceived such a fragrant odor, as of the fumes of frankincense or of some other precious spices.

38. So at length the lawless men, when they saw that the body could not be consumed by the fire, commanded an executioner to approach and pierce him with the sword.

39. And when he had done this there came forth a quantity of blood so that it extinguished the fire; and the whole crowd marveled that there should be such a difference between the unbelievers and the elect, of whom this man also was one, the most wonderful teacher in our times, apostolic and prophetic, who was bishop of the Catholic Church in Smyrna. For every word which came from his mouth was accomplished and will be accomplished.

40. But the jealous and envious Evil One, the adversary of the race of the righteous, when he saw the greatness

of his martyrdom, and his blameless life from the beginning, and when he saw him crowned with the crown of immortality and bearing off an incontestable prize, took care that not even his body should be taken away by us, although many desired to do it and to have communion with his holy flesh.

41. Accordingly certain ones secretly suggested to Nicetes, the father of Herod and brother of Alce, that he should plead with the magistrate not to give up his body, 'lest,' it was said, 'they should abandon the crucified One and begin to worship this man.' They said these things at the suggestion and impulse of the Jews, who also watched as we were about to take it from the fire, not knowing that we shall never be able either to forsake Christ, who suffered for the salvation of the whole world of those that are saved, or to worship any other.

42. For we worship him who is the Son of God, but the martyrs, as disciples and

imitators of the Lord, we love as they deserve on account of their matchless affection for their own king and teacher. May we also be made partakers and fellow-disciples with them.

43. The centurion, therefore, when he saw the contentiousness exhibited by the Jews, placed him in the midst and burned him, as was their custom. And so we afterwards gathered up his bones, which were more valuable than precious stones and more to be esteemed than gold, and laid them in a suitable place.

44. There the Lord will permit us to come together as we are able, in gladness and joy to celebrate the birthday of his martyrdom, for the commemoration of those who have already fought and for the training and preparation of those who shall hereafter do the same.

45. Such are the events that befell the blessed Polycarp, who suffered martyrdom in Smyrna with the eleven from Philadelphia.

This one man is remembered more than the others by all, so that even by the heathen he is talked about in every place.

46. Of such an end was the admirable and apostolic Polycarp deemed worthy, as recorded by the brethren of the church of Smyrna in their epistle which we have mentioned. In the same volume concerning him are subjoined also other martyrdoms which took place in the same city, Smyrna, about the same period of time with Polycarp's martyrdom. Among them also Metrodorus, who appears to have been a proselyte of the Marcionitic sect, suffered death by fire.

47. A celebrated martyr of those times was a certain man named Pionius. Those who desire to know his several confessions, and the boldness of his speech, and his apologies in behalf of the faith before the people and the rulers, and his instructive addresses and, moreover, his greetings to those who had yielded to temptation in the persecution, and the words of

encouragement which he addressed to the brethren who came to visit him in prison, and the tortures which he endured in addition, and besides these the sufferings and the nailings, and his firmness on the pile, and his death after all the extraordinary trials, – those we refer to that epistle which has been given in the Martyrdoms of the Ancients, collected by us, and which contains a very full account of him.

48. And there are also records extant of others that suffered martyrdom in Pergamus, a city of Asia – of Carpus and Papylus, and a woman named Agathonice, who, after many and illustrious testimonies, gloriously ended their lives.

CHAPTER SIXTEEN

Justin the Philosopher Preaches the Word of Christ in Rome and suffers Martyrdom

1. ABOUT THIS TIME JUSTIN, who was mentioned by us just above, after he had addressed a second work in behalf of our doctrines to the rulers already named, was crowned with divine martyrdom, in consequence of a plot laid against him by

Crescens, a philosopher who emulated the life and manners of the Cynics, whose name he bore. After Justin had frequently refuted him in public discussions he won by his martyrdom the prize of victory, dying in behalf of the truth which he preached.

2. And he himself, a man most learned in the truth, in his Apology already referred to clearly predicts how this was about to happen to him, although it had not yet occurred.

3. His words are as follows: I, too, therefore, expect to be plotted against and put in the stocks by some one of those whom I have named, or perhaps by Crescens, that unphilosophical and vainglorious man. For the man is not worthy to be called a philosopher who publicly bears witness against those concerning whom he knows nothing, declaring, for the sake of captivating and pleasing the multitude, that the Christians are atheistical and impious.

4. Doing this he errs greatly. For if he

assails us without having read the teachings of Christ, he is thoroughly depraved, and is much worse than the illiterate, who often guard against discussing and bearing false witness about matters which they do not understand. And if he has read them and does not understand the majesty that is in them, or, understanding it, does these things in order that he may not be suspected of being an adherent, he is far more base and totally depraved, being enslaved to vulgar applause and irrational fear.

5. For I would have you know that when I proposed certain questions of the sort and asked him in regard to them, I learned and proved that he indeed knows nothing. And to show that I speak the truth I am ready, if these disputations have not been reported to you, to discuss the questions again in your presence. And this indeed would be an act worthy of an emperor.

6. But if my questions and his answers have been made known to you, it is obvious

to you that he knows nothing about our affairs; or if he knows, but does not dare to speak because of those who hear him, he shows himself to be, as I have already said, not a philosopher, but a vainglorious man, who indeed does not even regard that most admirable saying of Socrates. These are the words of Justin.

7. And that he met his death as he had predicted that he would, in consequence of the machinations of Crescens, is stated by Tatian, a man who early in life lectured upon the sciences of the Greeks and won no little fame in them, and who has left a great many monuments of himself in his writings. He records this fact in his work against the Greeks, where he writes as follows: **"And that most admirable Justin declared with truth that the aforesaid persons were like robbers."**

8. Then, after making some remarks about the philosophers, he continues as follows: Crescens, indeed, who made his

nest in the great city, surpassed all in his unnatural lust, and was wholly devoted to the love of money.

9. And he who taught that death should be despised, was himself so greatly in fear of it that he endeavored to inflict death, as if it were a great evil, upon Justin, because the latter, when preaching the truth, had proved that the philosophers were gluttons and impostors. And such was the cause of Justin's martyrdom.

CHAPTER SEVENTEEN

The Martyrs whom Justin mentions in his Own Work

1. THE SAME MAN, before his conflict, mentions in his first Apology others that suffered martyrdom before him, and most fittingly records the following events.

2. He writes thus: A certain woman lived with a dissolute husband; she herself, too, having formerly been of the same character.

But when she came to the knowledge of the teachings of Christ, she became temperate, and endeavored to persuade her husband likewise to be temperate, repeating the teachings, and declaring the punishment in eternal fire which shall come upon those who do not live temperately and conformably to right reason.

3. But he, continuing in the same excesses, alienated his wife by his conduct. For she finally, thinking it wrong to live as a wife with a man who, contrary to the law of nature and right, sought every possible means of pleasure, desired to be divorced from him.

4. And when she was earnestly entreated by her friends, who counseled her still to remain with him, on the ground that her husband might some time give hope of amendment, she did violence to herself and remained.

5. But when her husband had gone to Alexandria, and was reported to be conducting himself still worse, she – in

order that she might not, by continuing in wedlock, and by sharing his board and bed, become a partaker in his lawlessness and impiety – gave him what we call a bill of divorce and left him.

6. But her noble and excellent husband – instead of rejoicing, as he ought to have done, that she had given up those actions which she had formerly recklessly committed with the servants and hirelings, when she delighted in drunkenness and in every vice, and that she desired him likewise to give them up – when she had gone from him contrary to his wish, brought an accusation concerning her, declaring that she was a Christian.

7. And she petitioned you, the emperor, that she might be permitted first to set her affairs in order, and afterwards, after the settlement of her affairs, to make her defense against the accusation. And this you granted.

8. But he who had once been her

husband, being no longer able to prosecute her, directed his attacks against a certain Ptolemæus, who had been her teacher in the doctrines of Christianity, and whom Urbicius had punished. Against him he proceeded in the following manner:

9. He persuaded a centurion who was his friend to cast Ptolemæus into prison, and to take him and ask him this only: was he a Christian? And when Ptolemæus, who was a lover of truth, and not of a deceitful and false disposition, confessed that he was a Christian, the centurion bound him and punished him for a long time in the prison.

10. And finally, when the man was brought before Urbicius he was likewise asked this question only: was he a Christian? And again, conscious of the benefits which he enjoyed through the teaching of Christ, he confessed his schooling in divine virtue.

11. For whoever denies that he is a Christian, either denies because he despises Christianity, or he avoids confession because

he is conscious that he is unworthy and an alien to it; neither of which is the case with the true Christian.

12. And when Urbicius commanded that he be led away to punishment, a certain Lucius, who was also a Christian, seeing judgment so unjustly passed, said to Urbicius, 'Why have you punished this man who is not an adulterer, nor a fornicator, nor a murderer, nor a thief, nor a robber, nor has been convicted of committing any crime at all, but has confessed that he bears the name of Christian? You do not judge, O Urbicius, in a manner befitting the Emperor Pius, or the philosophical son of Cæsar, or the sacred senate.'

13. And without making any other reply, he said to Lucius, 'You also seem to me to be one.' And when Lucius said, 'Certainly,' he again commanded that he too should be led away to punishment. But he professed his thanks, for he was liberated, he added, from such wicked rulers and was going to

the good Father and King, God. And still a third having come forward was condemned to be punished.

14. To this, Justin fittingly and consistently adds the words which we quoted above, saying, **"I, too, therefore expect to be plotted against by some one of those whom I have named,"** etc.

CHAPTER EIGHTEEN

The Works of Justin which have come down to us

1. THIS WRITER HAS LEFT us a great many monuments of a mind educated and practiced in divine things, which are replete with profitable matter of every kind. To them we shall refer the studious, noting as we proceed those that have come to our knowledge.

2. There is a certain discourse of his in

defense of our doctrine addressed to Antoninus surnamed the Pious, and to his sons, and to the Roman senate. Another work contains his second Apology in behalf of our faith, which he offered to him who was the successor of the emperor mentioned and who bore the same name, Antoninus Verus, the one whose times we are now recording.

3. Also another work against the Greeks, in which he discourses at length upon most of the questions at issue between us and the Greek philosophers, and discusses the nature of demons. It is not necessary for me to add any of these things here.

4. And still another work of his against the Greeks has come down to us, to which he gave the title Refutation. And besides these another, On the Sovereignty of God, which he establishes not only from our Scriptures, but also from the books of the Greeks.

5. Still further, a work entitled Psaltes, and another disputation On the Soul, in

which, after propounding various questions concerning the problem under discussion, he gives the opinions of the Greek philosophers, promising to refute it, and to present his own view in another work.

6. He composed also a dialogue against the Jews, which he held in the city of Ephesus with Trypho, a most distinguished man among the Hebrews of that day. In it he shows how the divine grace urged him on to the doctrine of the faith, and with what earnestness he had formerly pursued philosophical studies, and how ardent a search he had made for the truth.

7. And he records of the Jews in the same work, that they were plotting against the teaching of Christ, asserting the same things against Trypho: **"Not only did you not repent of the wickedness which you had committed, but you selected at that time chosen men, and you sent them out from Jerusalem through all the land, to announce that the godless**

heresy of the Christians had made its appearance, and to accuse them of those things which all that are ignorant of us say against us, so that you become the causes not only of your own injustice, but also of all other men's."

8. He writes also that even down to his time prophetic gifts shone in the Church. And he mentions the Apocalypse of John, saying distinctly that it was the apostle's. He also refers to certain prophetic declarations, and accuses Trypho on the ground that the Jews had cut them out of the Scripture. A great many other works of his are still in the hands of many of the brethren.

9. And the discourses of the man were thought so worthy of study even by the ancients, that Irenæus quotes his words: for instance, in the fourth book of his work Against Heresies, where he writes as follows: **"And Justin well says in his work against Marcion, that he would not have believed the Lord himself if he had preached**

another God besides the Creator"; and again in the fifth book of the same work he says: "**And Justin well said that before the coming of the Lord, Satan never dared to blaspheme God, because he did not yet know his condemnation.**"

10. These things I have deemed it necessary to say for the sake of stimulating the studious to peruse his works with diligence. So much concerning him.

CHAPTER NINETEEN

The Rulers of the Churches of Rome and Alexandria during the Reign of Verus

1. IN THE EIGHTH YEAR of the above-mentioned reign Soter succeeded Anicetus as bishop of the church of Rome, after the latter had held office eleven years in all. But when Celadion had presided over the church of Alexandria for fourteen years he was succeeded by Agripinnus.

CHAPTER TWENTY

The Rulers of the Church of Antioch

1. AT THAT TIME ALSO in the church of Antioch, Theophilus was well known as the sixth from the apostles. For Cornelius, who succeeded Hero, was the fourth, and after him Eros, the fifth in order, had held the office of bishop.

CHAPTER TWENTY ONE

The Ecclesiastical Writers that flourished in Those Days

1. AT THAT TIME THERE flourished in the Church Hegesippus, whom we know from what has gone before, and Dionysius, bishop of Corinth, and another bishop, Pinytus of Crete, and besides these, Philip, and Apolinarius, and Melito, and Musanus, and Modestus, and finally, Irenæus. From them has come down to us in writing, the

sound and orthodox faith received from apostolic tradition.

CHAPTER TWENTY TWO

Hegesippus and the Events which he mentions

1. HEGESIPPUS IN THE FIVE books of Memoirs which have come down to us has left a most complete record of his own views. In them he states that on a journey to Rome he met a great many bishops, and that he received the same doctrine from all. It is fitting to hear what he says after making some remarks about the epistle of Clement

to the Corinthians.

2. His words are as follows: And the church of Corinth continued in the true faith until Primus was bishop in Corinth. I conversed with them on my way to Rome, and abode with the Corinthians many days, during which we were mutually refreshed in the true doctrine.

3. And when I had come to Rome I remained there until Anicetus, whose deacon was Eleutherus. And Anicetus was succeeded by Soter, and he by Eleutherus. In every succession, and in every city that is held which is preached by the law and the prophets and the Lord.

4. The same author also describes the beginnings of the heresies which arose in his time, in the following words: And after James the Just had suffered martyrdom, as the Lord had also on the same account, Symeon, the son of the Lord's uncle, Clopas, was appointed the next bishop. All proposed him as second bishop because

he was a cousin of the Lord.

Therefore, they called the Church a virgin, for it was not yet corrupted by vain discourses.

5. But Thebuthis, because he was not made bishop, began to corrupt it. He also was sprung from the seven sects among the people, like Simon, from whom came the Simonians, and Cleobius, from whom came the Cleobians, and Dositheus, from whom came the Dositheans, and Gorthæus, from whom came the Goratheni, and Masbotheus, from whom came the Masbothæans. From them sprang the Menandrianists, and Marcionists, and Carpocratians, and Valentinians, and Basilidians, and Saturnilians. Each introduced privately and separately his own peculiar opinion. From them came false Christs, false prophets, false apostles, who divided the unity of the Church by corrupt doctrines uttered against God and against his Christ.

6. The same writer also records the ancient heresies which arose among the Jews, in the following words: **"There were, moreover, various opinions in the circumcision, among the children of Israel. The following were those that were opposed to the tribe of Judah and the Christ: Essenes, Galileans, Hemerobaptists,   Masbothæans, Samaritans, Sadducees, Pharisees."**

7. And he wrote of many other matters, which we have in part already mentioned, introducing the accounts in their appropriate places. And from the Syriac Gospel according to the Hebrews he quotes some passages in the Hebrew tongue, showing that he was a convert from the Hebrews, and he mentions other matters as taken from the unwritten tradition of the Jews.

8. And not only he, but also Irenæus and the whole company of the ancients, called the Proverbs of Solomon All-virtuous Wisdom. And when speaking of the books

called Apocrypha, he records that some of them were composed in his day by certain heretics. But let us now pass on to another.

CHAPTER TWENTY THREE

Dionysius, Bishop of Corinth, and the Epistles which he wrote

1. AND FIRST WE MUST speak of Dionysius, who was appointed bishop of the church in Corinth, and communicated freely of his inspired labors not only to his own people, but also to those in foreign lands, and rendered the greatest service to

all in the catholic epistles which he wrote to the churches.

2. Among these is the one addressed to the Lacedæmonians, containing instruction in the orthodox faith and an admonition to peace and unity; the one also addressed to the Athenians, exciting them to faith and to the life prescribed by the Gospel, which he accuses them of esteeming lightly, as if they had almost apostatized from the faith since the martyrdom of their ruler Publius, which had taken place during the persecutions of those days.

3. He mentions Quadratus also, stating that he was appointed their bishop after the martyrdom of Publius, and testifying that through his zeal they were brought together again and their faith revived. He records, moreover, that Dionysius the Areopagite, who was converted to the faith by the apostle Paul, according to the statement in the Acts of the Apostles, first obtained the episcopate of the church at

Athens.

4. And there is extant another epistle of his addressed to the Nicomedians, in which he attacks the heresy of Marcion, and stands fast by the canon of the truth.

5. Writing also to the church that is in Gortyna, together with the other parishes in Crete, he commends their bishop Philip, because of the many acts of fortitude which are testified to as performed by the church under him, and he warns them to be on their guard against the aberrations of the heretics.

6. And writing to the church that is in Amastris, together with those in Pontus, he refers to Bacchylides and Elpistus, as having urged him to write, and he adds explanations of passages of the divine Scriptures, and mentions their bishop Palmas by name. He gives them much advice also in regard to marriage and chastity, and commands them to receive those who come back again after any fall,

whether it be delinquency or heresy.

7. Among these is inserted also another epistle addressed to the Cnosians, in which he exhorts Pinytus, bishop of the parish, not to lay upon the brethren a grievous and compulsory burden in regard to chastity, but to have regard to the weakness of the multitude.

8. Pinytus, replying to this epistle, admires and commends Dionysius, but exhorts him in turn to impart some time more solid food, and to feed the people under him, when he wrote again, with more advanced teaching, that they might not be fed continually on these milky doctrines and imperceptibly grow old under a training calculated for children. In this epistle also Pinytus' orthodoxy in the faith and his care for the welfare of those placed under him, his learning and his comprehension of divine things, are revealed as in a most perfect image.

9. There is extant also another epistle written by Dionysius to the Romans, and

addressed to Soter, who was bishop at that time. We cannot do better than to subjoin some passages from this epistle, in which he commends the practice of the Romans which has been retained down to the persecution in our own days. His words are as follows:

10. **"For from the beginning it has been your practice to do good to all the brethren in various ways, and to send contributions to many churches in every city. Thus relieving the want of the needy, and making provision for the brethren in the mines by the gifts which you have sent from the beginning, you Romans keep up the hereditary customs of the Romans, which your blessed bishop Soter has not only maintained, but also added to, furnishing an abundance of supplies to the saints, and encouraging the brethren from abroad with blessed words, as a loving father his children."**

11. In this same epistle he makes mention also of Clement's epistle to the Corinthians,

showing that it had been the custom from the beginning to read it in the church. His words are as follows: **"Today we have passed the Lord's holy day, in which we have read your epistle. From it, whenever we read it, we shall always be able to draw advice, as also from the former epistle, which was written to us through Clement."**

12. The same writer also speaks as follows concerning his own epistles, alleging that they had been mutilated: **"As the brethren desired me to write epistles, I wrote. And these epistles the apostles of the devil have filled with tares, cutting out some things and adding others. For them a woe is reserved. It is, therefore, not to be wondered at if some have attempted to adulterate the Lord's writings also, since they have formed designs even against writings which are of less account."**

There is extant, in addition to these, another epistle of Dionysius, written to Chrysophora, a most faithful sister. In it he writes what is suitable, and imparts to her also the proper spiritual food. So much concerning Dionysius.

CHAPTER TWENTY FOUR
Theophilus Bishop of Antioch

1. OF THEOPHILUS, whom we have mentioned as bishop of the church of Antioch, three elementary works addressed to Autolycus are extant; also another writing entitled **Against the Heresy of Hermogenes**, in which he makes use of testimonies from the Apocalypse of John, and finally certain other catechetical books.

2. And as the heretics, no less then than

at other times, were like tares, destroying the pure harvest of apostolic teaching, the pastors of the churches everywhere hastened to restrain them as wild beasts from the fold of Christ, at one time by admonitions and exhortations to the brethren, at another time by contending more openly against them in oral discussions and refutations, and again by correcting their opinions with most accurate proofs in written works.

3. And that Theophilus also, with the others, contended against them, is manifest from a certain discourse of no common merit written by him against Marcion. This work too, with the others of which we have spoken, has been preserved to the present day.

Maximinus, the seventh from the apostles, succeeded him as bishop of the church of Antioch.

CHAPTER TWENTY FIVE

Philip and Modestus

PHILIP WHO, as we learn from the words of Dionysius, was bishop of the parish of Gortyna, likewise wrote a most elaborate work against Marcion, as did also Irenæus and Modestus. The last named has exposed the error of the man more clearly than the rest to the view of all. There are a number of others also whose works are still presented by a great many of the brethren.

CHAPTER TWENTY SIX

Melito and the Circumstances which he records

1. IN THOSE DAYS ALSO Melito, bishop of the parish in Sardis, and Apolinarius, bishop of Hierapolis, enjoyed great distinction. Each of them on his own part addressed apologies in behalf of the faith to the above-mentioned emperor of the Romans who was reigning at that time.

2. The following works of these writers have come to our knowledge. Of Melito, the

two books **On the Passover**, and one **On the Conduct of Life and the Prophets**, the discourse **On the Church**, and one **On the Lord's Day**, still further one **On the Faith of Man**, and one **On his Creation**, another also **On the Obedience of Faith**, and one **On the Senses**; besides these the work **On the Soul and Body**, and that **On Baptism**, and the one **On Truth**, and **On the Creation and Generation of Christ**; his discourse also **On Prophecy**, and that **On Hospitality**; still further, **The Key**, and the books **On the Devil and the Apocalypse of John**, and the work **On the Corporeality of God**, and finally the book addressed to Antoninus.

3. In the books **On the Passover** he indicatesthetimeatwhichhewrote,beginning with these words: **"While Servilius Paulus was proconsul of Asia, at the time when Sagaris suffered martyrdom, there arose in Laodicea a great strife concerning the Passover, which fell according to rule in**

those days; and these were written."

4. And Clement of Alexandria refers to this work in his own discourse **On the Passover**, which, he says, he wrote on occasion of Melito's work.

5. But in his book addressed to the emperor he records that the following events happened to us under him: **"For, what never before happened, the race of the pious is now suffering persecution, being driven about in Asia by new decrees. For the shameless informers and coveters of the property of others, taking occasion from the decrees, openly carry on robbery night and day, despoiling those who are guilty of no wrong."** And a little further on he says: If these things are done by your command, well and good. For a just ruler will never take unjust measures; and we indeed gladly accept the honor of such a death.

6. But this request alone we present to you, that you would yourself first examine the authors of such strife, and justly judge

whether they be worthy of death and punishment, or of safety and quiet. But if, on the other hand, this counsel and this new decree, which is not fit to be executed even against barbarian enemies, be not from you, much more do we beseech you not to leave us exposed to such lawless plundering by the populace.

7. Again he adds the following: For our philosophy formerly flourished among the Barbarians; but having sprung up among the nations under your rule, during the great reign of your ancestor Augustus, it became to your empire especially a blessing of auspicious omen. For from that time the power of the Romans has grown in greatness and splendor. To this power you have succeeded, as the desired possessor, and such shall you continue with your son, if you guard the philosophy which grew up with the empire and which came into existence with Augustus; that philosophy which your ancestors also honored along

with the other religions.

8. And a most convincing proof that our doctrine flourished for the good of an empire happily begun, is this – that there has no evil happened since Augustus' reign, but that, on the contrary, all things have been splendid and glorious, in accordance with the prayers of all.

9. Nero and Domitian, alone, persuaded by certain calumniators, have wished to slander our doctrine, and from them it has come to pass that the falsehood has been handed down, in consequence of an unreasonable practice which prevails of bringing slanderous accusations against the Christians.

10. But your pious fathers corrected their ignorance, having frequently rebuked in writing many who dared to attempt new measures against them. Among them your grandfather Adrian appears to have written to many others, and also to Fundanus, the proconsul and governor of Asia. And your

father, when you also were ruling with him, wrote to the cities, forbidding them to take any new measures against us; among the rest to the Larissæans, to the Thessalonians, to the Athenians, and to all the Greeks.

11. And as for you – since your opinions respecting the Christians are the same as theirs, and indeed much more benevolent and philosophic – we are the more persuaded that you will do all that we ask of you. These words are found in the above-mentioned work.

12. But in the Extracts made by him the same writer gives at the beginning of the introduction a catalogue of the acknowledged books of the Old Testament, which it is necessary to quote at this point. He writes as follows:

13. Melito to his brother Onesimus, greeting: Since you have often, in your zeal for the word, expressed a wish to have extracts made from the Law and the Prophets concerning the Saviour and

concerning our entire faith, and has also desired to have an accurate statement of the ancient book, as regards their number and their order, I have endeavored to perform the task, knowing your zeal for the faith, and your desire to gain information in regard to the word, and knowing that you, in your yearning after God, esteem these things above all else, struggling to attain eternal salvation.

14. Accordingly when I went East and came to the place where these things were preached and done, I learned accurately the books of the Old Testament, and send them to you as written below. Their names are as follows: Of Moses, five books: Genesis, Exodus, Numbers, Leviticus, Deuteronomy; Jesus Nave, Judges, Ruth; of Kings, four books; of Chronicles, two; the Psalms of David, the Proverbs of Solomon, Wisdom also, Ecclesiastes, Song of Songs, Job; of Prophets, Isaiah, Jeremiah; of the twelve prophets, one book ; Daniel, Ezekiel,

Esdras. From which also I have made the extracts, dividing them into six books. Such are the words of Melito.

CHAPTER TWENTY SEVEN

Apolinarius, Bishop of the Church of Hierapolis

A NUMBER OF WORKS of Apolinarius have been preserved by many, and the following have reached us: the Discourse addressed to the above-mentioned emperor, five books Against the Greeks, On Truth, a first and second book, and those which he subsequently wrote against the heresy of the Phrygians, which not long afterwards came out with its innovations, but at that time was, as it were, in its incipiency, since Montanus, with his false prophetesses, was then laying the foundations of his error.

CHAPTER TWENTY EIGHT

Musanus and His Writings

AND AS FOR MUSANUS, whom we have mentioned among the foregoing writers, a certain very elegant discourse is extant, which was written by him against some brethren that had gone over to the heresy of the so-called Encratites, which had recently sprung up, and which introduced a strange and pernicious error. It is said that Tatian was the author of this false doctrine.

CHAPTER TWENTY NINE
The Heresy of Tatian

1. HE IS THE ONE whose words we quoted a little above in regard to that admirable man, Justin, and whom we stated to have been a disciple of the martyr. Irenæus declares this in the first book of his work **Against Heresies**, where he writes as follows concerning both him and his heresy:

2. Those who are called Encratites, and who sprung from Saturninus and Marcion,

preached celibacy, setting aside the original arrangement of God and tacitly censuring him who made male and female for the propagation of the human race. They introduced also abstinence from the things called by them animate, thus showing ingratitude to the God who made all things. And they deny the salvation of the first man.

3. But this has been only recently discovered by them, a certain Tatian being the first to introduce this blasphemy. He was a hearer of Justin, and expressed no such opinion while he was with him, but after the martyrdom of the latter he left the Church, and becoming exalted with the thought of being a teacher, and puffed up with the idea that he was superior to others, he established a peculiar type of doctrine of his own, inventing certain invisible æons like the followers of Valentinus, while, like Marcion and Saturninus, he pronounced marriage to be corruption and fornication. His argument

against the salvation of Adam, however, he devised for himself. Irenæus at that time wrote thus.

4. But a little later a certain man named Severus put new strength into the aforesaid heresy, and thus brought it about that those who took their origin from it were called, after him, Severians.

5. They, indeed, use the Law and Prophets and Gospels, but interpret in their own way the utterances of the Sacred Scriptures. And they abuse Paul the apostle and reject his epistles, and do not accept even the Acts of the Apostles.

6. But their original founder, Tatian, formed a certain combination and collection of the Gospels, I know not how, to which he gave the title **Diatessaron**, and which is still in the hands of some. But they say that he ventured to paraphrase certain words of the apostle, in order to improve their style.

7. He has left a great many writings. Of these the one most in use among many

persons is his celebrated **Address to the Greeks**, which also appears to be the best and most useful of all his works. In it he deals with the most ancient times, and shows that Moses and the Hebrew prophets were older than all the celebrated men among the Greeks. So much in regard to these men.

CHAPTER THIRTY

Bardesanes the Syrian and his Extant Works

1. IN THE SAME REIGN, as heresies were abounding in the region between the rivers, a certain Bardesanes, a most able man and a most skillful disputant in the Syriac tongue, having composed dialogues against Marcion's followers and against certain others who were authors of various opinions, committed them to writing in his

own language, together with many other works. His pupils, of whom he had very many (for he was a powerful defender of the faith), translated these productions from the Syriac into Greek.

2. Among them there is also his most able dialogue **On Fate**, addressed to Antoninus, and other works which they say he wrote on occasion of the persecution which arose at that time.

3. He indeed was at first a follower of Valentinus, but afterward, having rejected his teaching and having refuted most of his fictions, he fancied that he had come over to the more correct opinion. Nevertheless he did not entirely wash off the filth of the old heresy.

About this time also Soter, bishop of the Church of Rome, departed this life.

BOOK FIVE

Introduction

1. SOTER, BISHOP OF THE church of
Rome, died after an episcopate of eight
years, and was succeeded by Eleutherus,
the twelfth from the apostles. In the
seventeenth year of the Emperor Antoninus
Verus, the persecution of our people was
rekindled more fiercely in certain districts

on account of an insurrection of the masses in the cities; and judging by the number in a single nation, myriads suffered martyrdom throughout the world. A record of this was written for posterity, and in truth it is worthy of perpetual remembrance.

2. A full account, containing the most reliable information on the subject, is given in our Collection of Martyrdoms, which constitutes a narrative instructive as well as historical. I will repeat here such portions of this account as may be needful for the present purpose.

3. Other writers of history record the victories of war and trophies won from enemies, the skill of generals, and the manly bravery of soldiers, defiled with blood and with innumerable slaughters for the sake of children and country and other possessions.

4. But our narrative of the government of God will record in ineffaceable letters the most peaceful wars waged in behalf of the peace of the soul, and will tell of men doing brave deeds for truth rather than country, and

for piety rather than dearest friends. It will hand down to imperishable remembrance the discipline and the much-tried fortitude of the athletes of religion, the trophies won from demons, the victories over invisible enemies, and the crowns placed upon all their heads.

The Number of those who fought for Religion in Gaul Under Verus and the Nature of their Conflicts

1. THE COUNTRY IN WHICH the arena was prepared for them was Gaul, of which Lyons and Vienne are the principal and most celebrated cities. The Rhone passes through both of them, flowing in a broad

stream through the entire region.

2. The most celebrated churches in that country sent an account of the witnesses to the churches in Asia and Phrygia, relating in the following manner what was done among them.

I will give their own words.

3. **"The servants of Christ residing at Vienne and Lyons, in Gaul, to the brethren through out Asia and Phrygia, who hold the same faith and hope of redemption, peace and grace and glory from God the Father and Christ Jesus our Lord."**

4. Then, having related some other matters, they begin their account in this manner: The greatness of the tribulation in this region, and the fury of the heathen against the saints, and the sufferings of the blessed witnesses, we cannot recount accurately, nor indeed could they possibly be recorded.

5. For with all his might the adversary fell upon us, giving us a foretaste of his

unbridled activity at his future coming. He endeavored in every manner to practice and exercise his servants against the servants of God, not only shutting us out from houses and baths and markets, but forbidding any of us to be seen in any place whatever.

6. But the grace of God led the conflict against him, and delivered the weak, and set them as firm pillars, able through patience to endure all the wrath of the Evil One. And they joined battle with him, undergoing all kinds of shame and injury; and regarding their great sufferings as little, they hastened to Christ, manifesting truly that 'the sufferings of this present time are not worthy to be compared with the glory which shall be revealed to us afterward.' Romans 8:18

7. First of all, they endured nobly the injuries heaped upon them by the populace; clamors and blows and draggings and robberies and stonings and imprisonments, and all things which an infuriated mob delight in inflicting

on enemies and adversaries.

8. Then, being taken to the forum by the chiliarch and the authorities of the city, they were examined in the presence of the whole multitude, and having confessed, they were imprisoned until the arrival of the governor.

9. When, afterwards, they were brought before him, and he treated us with the utmost cruelty, Vettius Epagathus, one of the brethren, and a man filled with love for God and his neighbor, interfered. His life was so consistent that, although young, he had attained a reputation equal to that of the elder Zacharias: for he 'walked in all the commandments and ordinances of the Lord blameless,' Luke 1:6 and was untiring in every good work for his neighbor, zealous for God and fervent in spirit. Such being his character, he could not endure the unreasonable judgment against us, but was filled with indignation, and asked to be permitted to testify in behalf of his brethren,

that there is among us nothing ungodly or impious.

10. But those about the judgment seat cried out against him, for he was a man of distinction; and the governor refused to grant his just request, and merely asked if he also were a Christian. And he, confessing this with a loud voice, was himself taken into the order of the witnesses, being called the Advocate of the Christians, but having the Advocate in himself, the Spirit more abundantly than Zacharias. He showed this by the fullness of his love, being well pleased even to lay down his life in defense of the brethren. For he was and is a true disciple of Christ, 'following the Lamb wherever he goes.' Revelation 14:4

11. Then the others were divided, [In Greek, διεκρίνοντο. Valesius finds in this word a figure taken from the athletic combats; for before the contests began the combatants were examined, and those found eligible were admitted (εἰσκρίνεσθαι), while the others were rejected (ἐκκρίνεσθαι).]

and the proto-witnesses were manifestly ready, and finished their confession with all eagerness. But some appeared unprepared and untrained, weak as yet, and unable to endure so great a conflict. About ten of these proved abortions, [The reading of ἐξέτρωσαν here is generally supported by scholars. Rufinus thought it should be ἐξέπεσον, which has perhaps a little stronger manuscript support. But Valesius points out that the former word is more unusual, and therefore more likely to have been changed into the latter by a copyist than the latter into the former.] causing us great grief and sorrow beyond measure, and impairing the zeal of the others who had not yet been seized, but who, though suffering all kinds of affliction, continued constantly with the witnesses and did not forsake them.

12. Then all of us feared greatly on account of uncertainty as to their confession; not because we dreaded the sufferings to be

endured, but because we looked to the end, and were afraid that some of them might fall away.

13. But those who were worthy were seized day by day, filling up their number, so that all the zealous persons, and those through whom especially our affairs had been established, were collected together out of the two churches.

14. And some of our heathen servants also were seized, as the governor had commanded that all of us should be examined publicly. These, being ensnared by Satan, and fearing for themselves the tortures which they beheld the saints endure, and being also urged on by the soldiers, accused us falsely of Thyestean banquets and Œdipodean intercourse, and of deeds which are not only unlawful for us to speak of or to think, but which we cannot believe were ever done by men.

15. When these accusations were reported, all the people raged like wild beasts against

us, so that even if any had before been moderate on account of friendship, they were now exceedingly furious and gnashed their teeth against us. And that which was spoken by our Lord was fulfilled: 'The time will come when whosoever kills you will think that he does God service.' John 16:2

16. Then finally the holy witnesses endured sufferings beyond description, Satan striving earnestly that some of the slanders might be uttered by them also.

17. But the whole wrath of the populace, and governor, and soldiers was aroused exceedingly against Sanctus, the deacon from Vienne, and Maturus, a late convert, yet a noble combatant, and against Attalus, a native of Pergamos where he had always been a pillar and foundation, and Blandina, through whom Christ showed that things which appear mean and obscure and despicable to men are with God of great glory, 1 Corinthians 1:27-28 through love toward him manifested in power, and not

boasting in appearance.

18. For while we all trembled, and her earthly mistress, who was herself also one of the witnesses, feared that on account of the weakness of her body, she would be unable to make bold confession, Blandina was filled with such power as to be delivered and raised above those who were torturing her by turns from morning till evening in every manner, so that they acknowledged that they were conquered, and could do nothing more to her. And they were astonished at her endurance, as her entire body was mangled and broken; and they testified that one of these forms of torture was sufficient to destroy life, not to speak of so many and so great sufferings.

19. But the blessed woman, like a noble athlete, renewed her strength in her confession; and her comfort and recreation and relief from the pain of her sufferings was in exclaiming, 'I am a Christian, and there is nothing vile done by us.'

20. But Sanctus also endured marvelously and superhumanly all the outrages which he suffered. While the wicked men hoped, by the continuance and severity of his tortures to wring something from him which he ought not to say, he girded himself against them with such firmness that he would not even tell his name, or the nation or city to which he belonged, or whether he was bond or free, but answered in the Roman tongue to all their questions, 'I am a Christian.' He confessed this instead of name and city and race and everything besides, and the people heard from him no other word.

21. There arose therefore on the part of the governor and his tormentors a great desire to conquer him; but having nothing more that they could do to him, they finally fastened red-hot brazen plates to the most tender parts of his body.

22. And these indeed were burned, but he continued unbending and unyielding, firm in his confession, and refreshed and

strengthened by the heavenly fountain of the water of life, flowing from the bowels of Christ.

23. And his body was a witness of his sufferings, being one complete wound and bruise, drawn out of shape, and altogether unlike a human form. Christ, suffering in him, manifested his glory, delivering him from his adversary, and making him an ensample for the others, showing that nothing is fearful where the love of the Father is, and nothing painful where there is the glory of Christ.

24. For when the wicked men tortured him a second time after some days, supposing that with his body swollen and inflamed to such a degree that he could not bear the touch of a hand, if they should again apply the same instruments, they would overcome him, or at least by his death under his sufferings others would be made afraid, not only did not this occur, but, contrary to all human expectation, his body arose and stood erect in the midst

of the subsequent torments, and resumed its original appearance and the use of its limbs, so that, through the grace of Christ, these second sufferings became to him, not torture, but healing.

25. But the devil, thinking that he had already consumed Biblias, who was one of those who had denied Christ, desiring to increase her condemnation through the utterance of blasphemy, brought her again to the torture, to compel her, as already feeble and weak, to report impious things concerning us.

26. But she recovered herself under the suffering, and as if awaking from a deep sleep, and reminded by the present anguish of the eternal punishment in hell, she contradicted the blasphemers. 'How,' she said, 'could those eat children who do not think it lawful to taste the blood even of irrational animals?' And thenceforward she confessed herself a Christian, and was given a place in the order of the witnesses.

27. But as the tyrannical tortures were made by Christ of none effect through the patience of the blessed, the devil invented other contrivances – confinement in the dark and most loathsome parts of the prison, stretching of the feet to the fifth hole in the stocks, and the other outrages which his servants are accustomed to inflict upon the prisoners when furious and filled with the devil. A great many were suffocated in prison, being chosen by the Lord for this manner of death, that he might manifest in them his glory.

28. For some, though they had been tortured so cruelly that it seemed impossible that they could live, even with the most careful nursing, yet, destitute of human attention, remained in the prison, being strengthened by the Lord, and invigorated both in body and soul; and they exhorted and encouraged the rest. But such as were young, and arrested recently, so that their bodies had not become accustomed to

torture, were unable to endure the severity of their confinement, and died in prison.

29. The blessed Pothinus, who had been entrusted with the bishopric of Lyons, was dragged to the judgment seat. He was more than ninety years of age, and very infirm, scarcely indeed able to breathe because of physical weakness; but he was strengthened by spiritual zeal through his earnest desire for martyrdom. Though his body was worn out by old age and disease, his life was preserved that Christ might triumph in it.

30. When he was brought by the soldiers to the tribunal, accompanied by the civil magistrates and a multitude who shouted against him in every manner as if he were Christ himself, he bore noble witness.

31. Being asked by the governor, Who was the God of the Christians, he replied, 'If you are worthy, you shall know.' Then he was dragged away harshly, and received blows of every kind. Those near him struck him with their hands and feet, regardless of

his age; and those at a distance hurled at him whatever they could seize; all of them thinking that they would be guilty of great wickedness and impiety if any possible abuse were omitted. For thus they thought to avenge their own deities. Scarcely able to breathe, he was cast into prison and died after two days.

32. Then a certain great dispensation of God occurred, and the compassion of Jesus appeared beyond measure, in a manner rarely seen among the brotherhood, but not beyond the power of Christ.

33. For those who had recanted at their first arrest were imprisoned with the others, and endured terrible sufferings, so that their denial was of no profit to them even for the present. But those who confessed what they were were imprisoned as Christians, no other accusation being brought against them. But the first were treated afterwards as murderers and defiled, and were punished twice as severely as the others.

34. For the joy of martyrdom, and the hope of the promises, and love for Christ, and the Spirit of the Father supported the latter; but their consciences so greatly distressed the former that they were easily distinguishable from all the rest by their very countenances when they were led forth.

35. For the first went out rejoicing, glory and grace being blended in their faces, so that even their bonds seemed like beautiful ornaments, as those of a bride adorned with variegated golden fringes; and they were perfumed with the sweet savor of Christ, so that some supposed they had been anointed with earthly ointment. But the others were downcast and humble and dejected and filled with every kind of disgrace, and they were reproached by the heathen as ignoble and weak, bearing the accusation of murderers, and having lost the one honorable and glorious and life-giving Name. The rest, beholding this, were strengthened,

and when apprehended, they confessed without hesitation, paying no attention to the persuasions of the devil.

36. After certain other words they continue:

After these things, finally, their martyrdoms were divided into every form. For plaiting a crown of various colors and of all kinds of flowers, they presented it to the Father. It was proper therefore that the noble athletes, having endured a manifold strife, and conquered grandly, should receive the crown, great and incorruptible.

37. Maturus, therefore, and Sanctus and Blandina and Attalus were led to the amphitheater to be exposed to the wild beasts, and to give to the heathen public a spectacle of cruelty, a day for fighting with wild beasts being specially appointed on account of our people.

38. Both Maturus and Sanctus passed again through every torment in the amphitheater, as if they had suffered nothing before, or rather, as if, having

already conquered their antagonist in many contests, they were now striving for the crown itself. They endured again the customary running of the gauntlet and the violence of the wild beasts, and everything which the furious people called for or desired, and at last, the iron chair in which their bodies being roasted, tormented them with the fumes.

39. And not with this did the persecutors cease, but were yet more mad against them, determined to overcome their patience. But even thus they did not hear a word from Sanctus except the confession which he had uttered from the beginning.

40. These, then, after their life had continued for a long time through the great conflict, were at last sacrificed, having been made throughout that day a spectacle to the world, in place of the usual variety of combats.

41. But Blandina was suspended on a stake, and exposed to be devoured by the

wild beasts who should attack her. And because she appeared as if hanging on a cross, and because of her earnest prayers, she inspired the combatants with great zeal. For they looked on her in her conflict, and beheld with their outward eyes, in the form of their sister, him who was crucified for them, that he might persuade those who believe in him, that every one who suffers for the glory of Christ has fellowship always with the living God.

42. As none of the wild beasts at that time touched her, she was taken down from the stake, and cast again into prison. She was preserved thus for another contest, that, being victorious in more conflicts, she might make the punishment of the crooked serpent irrevocable; and, though small and weak and despised, yet clothed with Christ the mighty and conquering Athlete, she might arouse the zeal of the brethren, and, having overcome the adversary many times might receive, through her conflict, the crown incorruptible.

43. But Attalus was called for loudly by the people, because he was a person of distinction. He entered the contest readily on account of a good conscience and his genuine practice in Christian discipline, and as he had always been a witness for the truth among us.

44. He was led around the amphitheater, a tablet being carried before him on which was written in the Roman language 'This is Attalus the Christian,' and the people were filled with indignation against him. But when the governor learned that he was a Roman, he commanded him to be taken back with the rest of those who were in prison concerning whom he had written to Cæsar, and whose answer he was awaiting.

45. But the intervening time was not wasted nor fruitless to them; for by their patience the measureless compassion of Christ was manifested. For through their continued life the dead were made alive, and the witnesses showed favor to those

who had failed to witness. And the virgin mother had much joy in receiving alive those whom she had brought forth as dead.

46. For through their influence many who had denied were restored, and re-begotten, and rekindled with life, and learned to confess. And being made alive and strengthened, they went to the judgment seat to be again interrogated by the governor; God, who desires not the death of the sinner, Ezekiel 33:11 but mercifully invites to repentance, treating them with kindness.

47. For Cæsar commanded that they should be put to death, but that any who might deny should be set free. Therefore, at the beginning of the public festival which took place there, and which was attended by crowds of men from all nations, the governor brought the blessed ones to the judgment seat, to make of them a show and spectacle for the multitude. Wherefore also he examined them again, and beheaded those who appeared to possess Roman

citizenship, but he sent the others to the wild beasts.

48. And Christ was glorified greatly in those who had formerly denied him, for, contrary to the expectation of the heathen, they confessed. For they were examined by themselves, as about to be set free; but confessing, they were added to the order of the witnesses. But some continued without, who had never possessed a trace of faith, nor any apprehension of the wedding garment, Matthew 22:11 nor an understanding of the fear of God; but, as sons of perdition, they blasphemed the Way through their apostasy.

49. But all the others were added to the Church. While these were being examined, a certain Alexander, a Phrygian by birth, and physician by profession, who had resided in Gaul for many years, and was well known to all on account of his love to God and boldness of speech (for he was not without a share of apostolic grace), standing

before the judgment seat, and by signs encouraging them to confess, appeared to those standing by as if in travail.

50. But the people being enraged because those who formerly denied now confessed, cried out against Alexander as if he were the cause of this. Then the governor summoned him and inquired who he was. And when he answered that he was a Christian, being very angry he condemned him to the wild beasts. And on the next day he entered along with Attalus. For to please the people, the governor had ordered Attalus again to the wild beasts.

51. And they were tortured in the amphitheater with all the instruments contrived for that purpose, and having endured a very great conflict, were at last sacrificed. Alexander neither groaned nor murmured in any manner, but communed in his heart with God.

52. But when Attalus was placed in the iron seat, and the fumes arose from his burning

body, he said to the people in the Roman language: 'Lo! This which you do is devouring men; but we do not devour men; nor do any other wicked thing.' And being asked, what name God has, he replied, 'God has not a name as man has.'

53. After all these, on the last day of the contests, Blandina was again brought in, with Ponticus, a boy about fifteen years old. They had been brought every day to witness the sufferings of the others, and had been pressed to swear by the idols. But because they remained steadfast and despised them, the multitude became furious, so that they had no compassion for the youth of the boy nor respect for the sex of the woman.

54. Therefore they exposed them to all the terrible sufferings and took them through the entire round of torture, repeatedly urging them to swear, but being unable to effect this; for Ponticus, encouraged by his sister so that even the heathen could see

that she was confirming and strengthening him, having nobly endured every torture, gave up the ghost.

55. But the blessed Blandina, last of all, having, as a noble mother, encouraged her children and sent them before her victorious to the King, endured herself all their conflicts and hastened after them, glad and rejoicing in her departure as if called to a marriage supper, rather than cast to wild beasts.

56. And, after the scourging, after the wild beasts, after the roasting seat, she was finally enclosed in a net, and thrown before a bull. And having been tossed about by the animal, but feeling none of the things which were happening to her, on account of her hope and firm hold upon what had been entrusted to her, and her communion with Christ, she also was sacrificed. And the heathen themselves confessed that never among them had a woman endured so many and such terrible tortures.

57. But not even thus was their madness

and cruelty toward the saints satisfied. For, incited by the Wild Beast, wild and barbarous tribes were not easily appeased, and their violence found another peculiar opportunity in the dead bodies.

58. For, through their lack of manly reason, the fact that they had been conquered did not put them to shame, but rather the more enkindled their wrath as that of a wild beast, and aroused alike the hatred of governor and people to treat us unjustly; that the Scripture might be fulfilled: 'He that is lawless, let him be lawless still, and he that is righteous, let him be righteous still.'

59. For they cast to the dogs those who had died of suffocation in the prison, carefully guarding them by night and day, lest any one should be buried by us. And they exposed the remains left by the wild beasts and by fire, mangled and charred, and placed the heads of the others by their bodies, and guarded them in like manner from burial by a watch of soldiers for many

days.

60. And some raged and gnashed their teeth against them, desiring to execute more severe vengeance upon them; but others laughed and mocked at them, magnifying their own idols, and imputed to them the punishment of the Christians. Even the more reasonable, and those who had seemed to sympathize somewhat, reproached them often, saying, 'Where is their God, and what has their religion, which they have chosen rather than life, profited them?'

61. So various was their conduct toward us; but we were in deep affliction because we could not bury the bodies. For neither did night avail us for this purpose, nor did money persuade, nor entreaty move to compassion; but they kept watch in every way, as if the prevention of the burial would be of some great advantage to them.

In addition, they say after other things:

62 . The bodies of the martyrs, having thus in every manner been exhibited and

exposed for six days, were afterward burned and reduced to ashes, and swept into the Rhone by the wicked men, so that no trace of them might appear on the earth.

63. And this they did, as if able to conquer God, and prevent their new birth; 'that,' as they said, 'they may have no hope of a resurrection, through trust in which they bring to us this foreign and new religion, and despise terrible things, and are ready even to go to death with joy. Now let us see if they will rise again, and if their God is able to help them, and to deliver them out of our hands.'

CHAPTER TWO

The Martyrs, beloved of God, kindly ministered unto those who fell in the Persecution

1. SUCH THINGS HAPPENED TO the churches of Christ under the above-mentioned emperor, from which we may reasonably conjecture the occurrences in the other provinces. It is proper to add other selections from the same letter, in

which the moderation and compassion of these witnesses is recorded in the following words:

2. They were also so zealous in their imitation of Christ –'who, being in the form of God, counted it not a prize to be on an equality with God,' Philippians 2:6 – that, though they had attained such honor, and had borne witness, not once or twice, but many times – having been brought back to prison from the wild beasts, covered with burns and scars and wounds – yet they did not proclaim themselves witnesses, nor did they suffer us to address them by this name. If any one of us, in letter or conversation, spoke of them as witnesses, they rebuked him sharply.

3. For they conceded cheerfully the appellation of Witness to Christ 'the faithful and true Witness,' Revelation 3:14 and 'firstborn of the dead,' Revelation 1:5 and prince of the life of God; and they reminded us of the witnesses who had already

departed, and said, 'They are already witnesses whom Christ has deemed worthy to be taken up in their confession, having sealed their testimony by their departure; but we are lowly and humble confessors.' And they besought the brethren with tears that earnest prayers should be offered that they might be made perfect.

4. They showed in their deeds the power of 'testimony,' manifesting great boldness toward all the brethren, and they made plain their nobility through patience and fearlessness and courage, but they refused the title of Witnesses as distinguishing them from their brethren, being filled with the fear of God.

5. A little further on they say: **"They humbled themselves under the mighty hand, by which they are now greatly exalted. They defended all, but accused none. They absolved all, but bound none. And they prayed for those who had inflicted cruelties upon them, even as**

Stephen, the perfect witness, 'Lord, lay not this sin to their charge.' Acts 7:60 But if he prayed for those who stoned him, how much more for the brethren!"

6. And again after mentioning other matters, they say:

For, through the genuineness of their love, their greatest contest with him was that the Beast, being choked, might cast out alive those whom he supposed he had swallowed. For they did not boast over the fallen, but helped them in their need with those things in which they themselves abounded, having the compassion of a mother, and shedding many tears on their account before the Father.

7. They asked for life, and he gave it to them, and they shared it with their neighbors. Victorious over everything, they departed to God. Having always loved peace, and having commended peace to us they went in peace to God, leaving no sorrow to their mother, nor division or strife to the brethren, but joy

and peace and concord and love.

8. This record of the affection of those blessed ones toward the brethren that had fallen may be profitably added on account of the inhuman and unmerciful disposition of those who, after these events, acted unsparingly toward the members of Christ.

CHAPTER THREE

The Vision which appeared in a
Dream to the Witness Attalus

1. THE SAME LETTER OF the above-mentioned witnesses contains another account worthy of remembrance. No one will object to our bringing it to the knowledge of our readers.

2. It runs as follows: For a certain Alcibiades, who was one of them, led a very austere life, partaking of nothing whatever

517

but bread and water. When he endeavored to continue this same sort of life in prison, it was revealed to Attalus after his first conflict in the amphitheater that Alcibiades was not doing well in refusing the creatures of God and placing a stumbling-block before others.

3. And Alcibiades obeyed, and partook of all things without restraint, giving thanks to God. For they were not deprived of the grace of God, but the Holy Ghost was their counselor. Let this suffice for these matters.

4. The followers of Montanus, Alcibiades and Theodotus in Phrygia were now first giving wide circulation to their assumption in regard to prophecy – for the many other miracles that, through the gift of God, were still wrought in the different churches caused their prophesying to be readily credited by many – and as dissension arose concerning them, the brethren in Gaul set forth their own prudent and most orthodox judgment

in the matter, and published also several epistles from the witnesses that had been put to death among them. These they sent, while they were still in prison, to the brethren throughout Asia and Phrygia, and also to Eleutherus, who was then bishop of Rome, negotiating for the peace of the churches.

CHAPTER FOUR

Irenæus commended by the Witnesses in a Letter

1. THE SAME WITNESSES ALSO recommended Irenæus, who was already at that time a presbyter of the parish of Lyons, to the above-mentioned bishop of Rome, saying many favorable things in regard to him, as the following extract shows:

2. "We pray, father Eleutherus, that you may rejoice in God in all things and

always. We have requested our brother and comrade Irenæus to carry this letter to you, and we ask you to hold him in esteem, as zealous for the covenant of Christ. For if we thought that office could confer righteousness upon any one, we should commend him among the first as a presbyter of the church, which is his position."

3. Why should we transcribe the catalogue of the witnesses given in the letter already mentioned, of whom some were beheaded, others cast to the wild beasts, and others fell asleep in prison, or give the number of confessors still surviving at that time? For whoever desires can readily find the full account by consulting the letter itself, which, as I have said, is recorded in our Collection of Martyrdoms. Such were the events which happened under Antoninus.

CHAPTER FIVE

God sent Rain from Heaven for Marcus Aurelius Cæsar in Answer to the Prayers of our People

1. IT IS REPORTED THAT Marcus Aurelius Cæsar, brother of Antoninus, being about to engage in battle with the Germans and Sarmatians, was in great trouble on account of his army suffering

from thirst. But the soldiers of the so-called Melitene legion, through the faith which has given strength from that time to the present, when they were drawn up before the enemy, kneeled on the ground, as is our custom in prayer, and engaged in supplications to God.

2. This was indeed a strange sight to the enemy, but it is reported that a stranger thing immediately followed. The lightning drove the enemy to flight and destruction, but a shower refreshed the army of those who had called on God, all of whom had been on the point of perishing with thirst.

3. This story is related by non-Christian writers who have been pleased to treat the times referred to, and it has also been recorded by our own people. By those historians who were strangers to the faith, the marvel is mentioned, but it is not acknowledged as an answer to our prayers. But by our own people, as friends of the truth, the occurrence is related in a

simple and artless manner.

4. Among these is Apolinarius, who says that from that time the legion through whose prayers the wonder took place received from the emperor a title appropriate to the event, being called in the language of the Romans the Thundering Legion.

5. Tertullian is a trustworthy witness of these things. In the Apology for the Faith, which he addressed to the Roman Senate, and which work we have already mentioned, he confirms the history with greater and stronger proofs.

6. He writes that there are still extant letters of the most intelligent Emperor Marcus in which he testifies that his army, being on the point of perishing with thirst in Germany, was saved by the prayers of the Christians. And he says also that this emperor threatened death to those who brought accusation against us.

7. He adds further:

"What kind of laws are those which

impious, unjust, and cruel persons use against us alone? Which Vespasian, though he had conquered the Jews, did not regard; which Trajan partially annulled, forbidding Christians to be sought after; which neither Adrian, though inquisitive in all matters, nor he who was called Pius sanctioned." But let any one treat these things as he chooses; we must pass on to what followed.

8. Pothinus having died with the other martyrs in Gaul at ninety years of age, Irenæus succeeded him in the episcopate of the church at Lyons. We have learned that, in his youth, he was a hearer of Polycarp.

9. In the third book of his work Against Heresies he has inserted a list of the bishops of Rome, bringing it down as far as Eleutherus (whose times we are now considering), under whom he composed his work. He writes as follows:

CHAPTER SIX

Catalogue of the
Bishops of Rome

1. THE BLESSED APOSTLES HAVING founded and established the church, entrusted the office of the episcopate to Linus. Paul speaks of this Linus in his Epistles to Timothy. 2 Timothy 4:21

2. Anencletus succeeded him, and after Anencletus, in the third place from the apostles, Clement received the episcopate.

He had seen and conversed with the blessed apostles, and their preaching was still sounding in his ears, and their tradition was still before his eyes. Nor was he alone in this, for many who had been taught by the apostles yet survived.

3. In the times of Clement, a serious dissension having arisen among the brethren in Corinth, the church of Rome sent a most suitable letter to the Corinthians, reconciling them in peace, renewing their faith, and proclaiming the doctrine lately received from the apostles.

4. A little farther on he says:

Evarestus succeeded Clement, and Alexander, Evarestus. Then Xystus, the sixth from the apostles, was appointed. After him Telesphorus, who suffered martyrdom gloriously; then Hyginus; then Pius; and after him Anicetus; Soter succeeded Anicetus; and now, in the twelfth place from the apostles, Eleutherus holds the office of bishop.

5. In the same order and succession the

tradition in the Church and the preaching of the truth has descended from the apostles unto us.

CHAPTER SEVEN

Even down to those Times Miracles were performed by the Faithful

1. THESE THINGS IRENÆUS, in agreement with the accounts already given by us, records in the work which comprises five books, and to which he gave the title Refutation and Overthrow of the Knowledge Falsely So-called. In the second book of the

same treatise he shows that manifestations of divine and miraculous power continued to his time in some of the churches.

2. He says:

"But so far do they come short of raising the dead, as the Lord raised them, and the apostles through prayer. And oftentimes in the brotherhood, when, on account of some necessity, our entire Church has besought with fasting and much supplication, the spirit of the dead has returned, and the man has been restored through the prayers of the saints."

3. And again, after other remarks, he says:

If they will say that even the Lord did these things in mere appearance, we will refer them to the prophetic writings, and show from them that all things were beforehand spoken of him in this manner, and were strictly fulfilled; and that he alone is the Son of God. Wherefore his true disciples, receiving grace from him, perform such works in his Name for the benefit of other men, as each has received the gift from him.

4. For some of them drive out demons effectually and truly, so that those who have been cleansed from evil spirits frequently believe and unite with the Church. Others have a foreknowledge of future events, and visions, and prophetic revelations. Still others heal the sick by the laying on of hands, and restore them to health. And, as we have said, even dead persons have been raised, and remained with us many years.

5. But why should we say more? It is not possible to recount the number of gifts which the Church, throughout all the world, has received from God in the name of Jesus Christ, who was crucified under Pontius Pilate, and exercises every day for the benefit of the heathen, never deceiving any nor doing it for money. For as she has received freely from God, freely also does she minister.

6. And in another place the same author writes:

"**As also we hear that many brethren in the Church possess prophetic gifts, and speak, through the Spirit, with all kinds of tongues, and bring to light the secret things of men for their good, and declare the mysteries of God.**"

So much in regard to the fact that various gifts remained among those who were worthy even until that time.

CHAPTER EIGHT

The Statements of Irenæus in regard to the Divine Scriptures

1. SINCE, IN THE BEGINNING of this work, we promised to give, when needful, the words of the ancient presbyters and writers of the Church, in which they have declared those traditions which came down to them concerning the canonical books, and since Irenæus was one of them, we will now give his words and, first, what he

533

says of the sacred Gospels:

2. Matthew published his Gospel among the Hebrews in their own language, while Peter and Paul were preaching and founding the church in Rome.

3. After their departure Mark, the disciple and interpreter of Peter, also transmitted to us in writing those things which Peter had preached; and Luke, the attendant of Paul, recorded in a book the Gospel which Paul had declared.

4. Afterwards John, the disciple of the Lord, who also reclined on his bosom, published his Gospel, while staying at Ephesus in Asia.

5. He states these things in the third book of his above-mentioned work. In the fifth book he speaks as follows concerning the Apocalypse of John, and the number of the name of Antichrist:

"As these things are so, and this number is found in all the approved and ancient copies, and those who saw

John face to face confirm it, and reason teaches us that the number of the name of the beast, according to the mode of calculation among the Greeks, appears in its letters...."

6. And further on he says concerning the same:

"We are not bold enough to speak confidently of the name of Antichrist. For if it were necessary that his name should be declared clearly at the present time, it would have been announced by him who saw the revelation. For it was seen, not long ago, but almost in our generation, toward the end of the reign of Domitian."

7. He states these things concerning the Apocalypse in the work referred to. He also mentions the first Epistle of John, taking many proofs from it, and likewise the first Epistle of Peter. And he not only knows, but also receives, The Shepherd, writing as follows:

"Well did the Scripture speak, saying, 'First of all believe that God is one, who has created and completed all things,'" etc.

8. And he uses almost the precise words of the Wisdom of Solomon, saying: **"The vision of God produces immortality, but immortality renders us near to God."** He mentions also the memoirs of a certain apostolic presbyter, whose name he passes by in silence, and gives his expositions of the sacred Scriptures.

9. And he refers to Justin the Martyr, and to Ignatius, using testimonies also from their writings. Moreover, he promises to refute Marcion from his own writings, in a special work.

10. Concerning the translation of the inspired Scriptures by the Seventy, hear the very words which he writes:

"God in truth became man, and the Lord himself saved us, giving the sign of the virgin; but not as some say, who

now venture to translate the Scripture, 'Behold, a young woman shall conceive and bring forth a son,' as Theodotion of Ephesus and Aquila of Pontus, both of them Jewish proselytes, interpreted; following whom, the Ebionites say that he was begotten by Joseph."

11. Shortly after he adds:

For before the Romans had established their empire, while the Macedonians were still holding Asia, Ptolemy, the son of Lagus, being desirous of adorning the library which he had founded in Alexandria with the meritorious writings of all men, requested the people of Jerusalem to have their Scriptures translated into the Greek language.

12. But, as they were then subject to the Macedonians, they sent to Ptolemy seventy elders, who were the most skilled among them in the Scriptures and in both languages. Thus God accomplished his purpose.

13. But wishing to try them individually, as he feared lest, by taking counsel together, they might conceal the truth of the Scriptures by their interpretation, he separated them from one another, and commanded all of them to write the same translation. He did this for all the books.

14. But when they came together in the presence of Ptolemy, and compared their several translations, God was glorified, and the Scriptures were recognized as truly divine. For all of them had rendered the same things in the same words and with the same names from beginning to end, so that the heathen perceived that the Scriptures had been translated by the inspiration of God.

15. And this was nothing wonderful for God to do, who, in the captivity of the people under Nebuchadnezzar, when the Scriptures had been destroyed, and the Jews had returned to their own country after seventy years, afterwards, in the time of Artaxerxes, king of the Persians, inspired

Ezra the priest, of the tribe of Levi, to relate all the words of the former prophets, and to restore to the people the legislation of Moses.

Such are the words of Irenæus.

CHAPTER NINE
The Bishops under Commodus

1. AFTER ANTONINUS HAD BEEN emperor for nineteen years, Commodus received the government. In his first year Julian became bishop of the Alexandrian churches, after Agripinnus had held the office for twelve years.

CHAPTER TEN

Pantænus the Philosopher

1. ABOUT THAT TIME, Pantænus, a man highly distinguished for his learning, had charge of the school of the faithful in Alexandria. A school of sacred learning, which continues to our day, was established there in ancient times, and as we have been informed, was managed by men of great ability and zeal for divine things. Among these it is reported that Pantænus was at

that time especially conspicuous, as he had been educated in the philosophical system of those called Stoics.

2. They say that he displayed such zeal for the divine Word, that he was appointed as a herald of the Gospel of Christ to the nations in the East, and was sent as far as India. For indeed there were still many evangelists of the Word who sought earnestly to use their inspired zeal, after the examples of the apostles, for the increase and building up of the Divine Word.

3. Pantænus was one of these, and is said to have gone to India. It is reported that among persons there who knew of Christ, he found the Gospel according to Matthew, which had anticipated his own arrival. For Bartholomew, one of the apostles, had preached to them, and left with them the writing of Matthew in the Hebrew language, which they had preserved till that time.

4. After many good deeds, Pantænus finally became the head of the school at

Alexandria, and expounded the treasures of divine doctrine both orally and in writing.

CHAPTER ELEVEN
Clement of Alexandria

1. AT THIS TIME Clement, being trained with him in the divine Scriptures at Alexandria, became well known. He had the same name as the one who anciently was at the head of the Roman church, and who was a disciple of the apostles.

2. In his Hypotyposes he speaks of Pantænus by name as his teacher. It seems to me that he alludes to the same person

also in the first book of his Stromata, when, referring to the more conspicuous of the successors of the apostles whom he had met, he says:

3. This work is not a writing artfully constructed for display; but my notes are stored up for old age, as a remedy against forgetfulness; an image without art, and a rough sketch of those powerful and animated words which it was my privilege to hear, as well as of blessed and truly remarkable men.

4. Of these the one – the Ionian – was in Greece, the other in Magna Græcia; the one of them was from Cœle-Syria, the other from Egypt. There were others in the East, one of them an Assyrian, the other a Hebrew in Palestine. But when I met with the last, – in ability truly he was first – having hunted him out in his concealment in Egypt, I found rest.

5. These men, preserving the true tradition of the blessed doctrine, directly from the

holy apostles, Peter and James and John and Paul, the son receiving it from the father (but few were like the fathers), have come by God's will even to us to deposit those ancestral and apostolic seeds.

CHAPTER TWELVE
The Bishops in Jerusalem

1. AT THIS TIME NARCISSUS was the bishop of the church at Jerusalem, and he is celebrated by many to this day. He was the fifteenth in succession from the siege of the Jews under Adrian. We have shown that from that time first the church in Jerusalem was composed of Gentiles, after those of the circumcision, and that Marcus was the first Gentile bishop that presided over them.

2. After him the succession in the episcopate was: first Cassianus; after him Publius; then Maximus; following them Julian; then Gaius; after him Symmachus and another Gaius, and again another Julian; after these Capito and Valens and Dolichianus; and after all of them Narcissus, the thirtieth in regular succession from the apostles.

CHAPTER THIRTEEN

Rhodo and his Account of the Dissension of Marcion

1. AT THIS TIME RHODO, a native of Asia, who had been instructed, as he himself states, by Tatian, with whom we have already become acquainted, having written several books, published among the rest one against the heresy of Marcion. He says that this heresy was divided in his time into various opinions; and while describing those

who occasioned the division, he refutes accurately the falsehoods devised by each of them.

2. But hear what he writes:

Therefore also they disagree among themselves, maintaining an inconsistent opinion. For Apelles, one of the herd, priding himself on his manner of life and his age, acknowledges one principle, but says that the prophecies are from an opposing spirit, being led to this view by the responses of a maiden by name Philumene, who was possessed by a demon.

3. But others, among whom are Potitus and Basilicus, hold to two principles, as does the mariner Marcion himself.

4. These following the wolf of Pontus, and, like him, unable to fathom the division of things, became reckless, and without giving any proof asserted two principles. Others, again, drifting into a worse error, consider that there are not only two, but three natures. Of these, Syneros is the leader and chief, as

those who defend his teaching say.

5. The same author writes that he engaged in conversation with Apelles. He speaks as follows:

"For the old man Apelles, when conversing with us, was refuted in many things which he spoke falsely; whence also he said that it was not at all necessary to examine one's doctrine, but that each one should continue to hold what he believed. For he asserted that those who trusted in the Crucified would be saved, if only they were found doing good works. But as we have said before, his opinion concerning God was the most obscure of all. For he spoke of one principle, as also our doctrine does."

6. Then, after stating fully his own opinion, he adds:

When I said to him, Tell me how you know this or how can you assert that there is one principle, he replied that the prophecies refuted themselves, because they have said nothing true; for they are inconsistent, and false, and self-contradictory. But how there is one principle he said that he did not know, but that he was thus persuaded.

7. As I then adjured him to speak the truth, he swore that he did so when he said that he did not know how there is one unbegotten God, but that he believed it. Thereupon I laughed and reproved him because, though calling himself a teacher, he knew not how to confirm what he taught.

8. In the same work, addressing Callistio, the same writer acknowledges that he had been instructed at Rome by Tatian. And he says that a book of Problems had been prepared by Tatian, in which he promised to explain the obscure and hidden parts of the divine Scriptures. Rhodo himself promises to give in a work of his own solutions of Tatian's problems. There is also extant a Commentary of his on the Hexæmeron.

9. But this Apelles wrote many things, in

an impious manner, of the law of Moses, blaspheming the divine words in many of his works, being, as it seemed, very zealous for their refutation and overthrow.

So much concerning these.

CHAPTER FOURTEEN

The False Prophets of the Phrygians

THE ENEMY OF GOD'S Church, who is emphatically a hater of good and a lover of evil, and leaves untried no manner of craft against men, was again active in causing strange heresies to spring up against the Church. For some persons, like venomous reptiles, crawled over Asia and Phrygia, boasting that Montanus was the Paraclete, and that the women that followed him, Priscilla and Maximilla, were prophetesses of Montanus.

CHAPTER FIFTEEN

The Schism of Blastus at Rome

OTHERS, OF WHOM FLORINUS was
chief, flourished at Rome. He fell from the
presbyterate of the Church, and Blastus was
involved in a similar fall. They also drew away
many of the Church to their opinion, each
striving to introduce his own innovations in
respect to the truth.

556

CHAPTER SIXTEEN

The Circumstances related of Montanus and his False Prophets

1. AGAINST THE SO-CALLED Phrygian heresy, the power which always contends for the truth raised up a strong and invincible weapon, Apolinarius of Hierapolis, whom we have mentioned before, and with him many other men of ability, by whom abundant material for our history has been left.

2. A certain one of these, in the beginning

of his work against them, first intimates that he had contended with them in oral controversies.

3. He commences his work in this manner:

Having for a very long and sufficient time, O beloved Avircius Marcellus, been urged by you to write a treatise against the heresy of those who are called after Miltiades, I have hesitated till the present time, not through lack of ability to refute the falsehood or bear testimony for the truth, but from fear and apprehension that I might seem to some to be making additions to the doctrines or precepts of the Gospel of the New Testament, which it is impossible for one who has chosen to live according to the Gospel, either to increase or to diminish.

4. But being recently in Ancyra in Galatia, I found the church there greatly agitated by this novelty, not prophecy, as they call it, but rather false prophecy, as will be shown. Therefore, to the best of our ability, with the Lord's help, we disputed in the church many

days concerning these and other matters separately brought forward by them, so that the church rejoiced and was strengthened in the truth, and those of the opposite side were for the time confounded, and the adversaries were grieved.

5. The presbyters in the place, our fellow presbyter Zoticus of Otrous also being present, requested us to leave a record of what had been said against the opposers of the truth. We did not do this, but we promised to write it out as soon as the Lord permitted us, and to send it to them speedily.

6. Having said this with other things, in the beginning of his work, he proceeds to state the cause of the above-mentioned heresy as follows:

Their opposition and their recent heresy which has separated them from the Church arose on the following account.

7. There is said to be a certain village called Ardabau in that part of Mysia, which

borders upon Phrygia. There first, they say, when Gratus was proconsul of Asia, a recent convert, Montanus by name, through his unquenchable desire for leadership, gave the adversary opportunity against him. And he became beside himself, and being suddenly in a sort of frenzy and ecstasy, he raved, and began to babble and utter strange things, prophesying in a manner contrary to the constant custom of the Church handed down by tradition from the beginning.

8. Some of those who heard his spurious utterances at that time were indignant, and they rebuked him as one that was possessed, and that was under the control of a demon, and was led by a deceitful spirit, and was distracting the multitude; and they forbade him to talk, remembering the distinction drawn by the Lord and his warning to guard watchfully against the coming of false prophets. Matthew 7:15 But others imagining themselves possessed of the Holy Spirit and of a prophetic gift,

were elated and not a little puffed up; and forgetting the distinction of the Lord, they challenged the mad and insidious and seducing spirit, and were cheated and deceived by him. In consequence of this, he could no longer be held in check, so as to keep silence.

9. Thus by artifice, or rather by such a system of wicked craft, the devil, devising destruction for the disobedient, and being unworthily honored by them, secretly excited and inflamed their understandings which had already become estranged from the true faith. And he stirred up besides two women, and filled them with the false spirit, so that they talked wildly and unreasonably and strangely, like the person already mentioned. And the spirit pronounced them blessed as they rejoiced and gloried in him, and puffed them up by the magnitude of his promises. But sometimes he rebuked them openly in a wise and faithful manner, that he might seem to be a reprover. But those

of the Phrygians that were deceived were few in number.

And the arrogant spirit taught them to revile the entire universal Church under heaven, because the spirit of false prophecy received neither honor from it nor entrance into it.

10. For the faithful in Asia met often in many places throughout Asia to consider this matter, and examined the novel utterances and pronounced them profane, and rejected the heresy, and thus these persons were expelled from the Church and debarred from communion.

11. Having related these things at the outset, and continued the refutation of their delusion through his entire work, in the second book he speaks as follows of their end:

12. Since, therefore, they called us slayers of the prophets because we did not receive their loquacious prophets, who, they say, are those that the Lord promised

to send to the people, Matthew 23:34 let them answer as in God's presence: Who is there, O friends, of these who began to talk, from Montanus and the women down, that was persecuted by the Jews, or slain by lawless men? None. Or has any of them been seized and crucified for the Name? Truly not. Or has one of these women ever been scourged in the synagogues of the Jews, or stoned? No; never anywhere.

13. But by another kind of death Montanus and Maximilla are said to have died. For the report is that, incited by the spirit of frenzy, they both hung themselves; not at the same time, but at the time which common report gives for the death of each. And thus they died, and ended their lives like the traitor Judas.

14. So also, as general report says, that remarkable person, the first steward, as it were, of their so-called prophecy, one Theodotus – who, as if at sometime taken up and received into heaven, fell into trances,

and entrusted himself to the deceitful spirit – was pitched like a quoit, and died miserably.

15. They say that these things happened in this manner. But as we did not see them, O friend, we do not pretend to know. Perhaps in such a manner, perhaps not, Montanus and Theodotus and the above-mentioned woman died.

16. He says again in the same book that the holy bishops of that time attempted to refute the spirit in Maximilla, but were prevented by others who plainly co-operated with the spirit.

17. He writes as follows:

"And let not the spirit, in the same work of Asterius Urbanus, say through Maximilla, 'I am driven away from the sheep like a wolf. I am not a wolf. I am word and spirit and power.' But let him show clearly and prove the power in the spirit. And by the spirit let him compel those to confess him who were then present for the purpose of proving and

reasoning with the talkative spirit, – those eminent men and bishops, Zoticus, from the village Comana, and Julian, from Apamea, whose mouths the followers of Themiso muzzled, refusing to permit the false and seductive spirit to be refuted by them."

18. Again in the same work, after saying other things in refutation of the false prophecies of Maximilla, he indicates the time when he wrote these accounts, and mentions her predictions in which she prophesied wars and anarchy. Their falsehood he censures in the following manner:

19. **"And has not this been shown clearly to be false? For it is today more than thirteen years since the woman died, and there has been neither a partial nor general war in the world; but rather, through the mercy of God, continued peace even to the Christians."** These things are taken from the second book.

20. I will add also short extracts from the third book, in which he speaks thus against their boasts that many of them had suffered martyrdom:

When therefore they are at a loss, being refuted in all that they say, they try to take refuge in their martyrs, alleging that they have many martyrs, and that this is sure evidence of the power of the so-called prophetic spirit that is with them. But this, as it appears, is entirely fallacious.

21. For some of the heresies have a great many martyrs; but surely we shall not on that account agree with them or confess that they hold the truth. And first, indeed, those called Marcionites, from the heresy of Marcion, say that they have a multitude of martyrs for Christ; yet they do not confess Christ himself in truth.

A little farther on he continues:

22. **"When those called to martyrdom from the Church for the truth of the faith have met with any of the so-called**

martyrs of the Phrygian heresy, they have separated from them, and died without any fellowship with them, because they did not wish to give their assent to the spirit of Montanus and the women. And that this is true and took place in our own time in Apamea on the Mæander, among those who suffered martyrdom with Gaius and Alexander of Eumenia, is well known."

CHAPTER SEVENTEEN

Miltiades and His Works

1. IN THIS WORK HE mentions a writer, Miltiades, stating that he also wrote a certain book against the above-mentioned heresy. After quoting some of their words, he adds: **"Having found these things in a certain work of theirs in opposition to the work of the brother Alcibiades, in which he shows that a prophet ought not to speak in ecstasy, I made an abridgment."**

568

2. A little further on in the same work he gives a list of those who prophesied under the new covenant, among whom he enumerates a certain Ammia and Quadratus, saying:

But the false prophet falls into an ecstasy, in which he is without shame or fear. Beginning with purposed ignorance, he passes on, as has been stated, to involuntary madness of soul.

3. They cannot show that one of the old or one of the new prophets was thus carried away in spirit. Neither can they boast of Agabus, or Judas, or Silas, or the daughters of Philip, or Ammia in Philadelphia, or Quadratus, or any others not belonging to them.

4. And again after a little he says: **"For if after Quadratus and Ammia in Philadelphia, as they assert, the women with Montanus received the prophetic gift, let them show who among them received it from Montanus and the women. For the apostle thought it necessary that the prophetic**

gift should continue in all the Church until the final coming. But they cannot show it, though this is the fourteenth year since the death of Maximilla."

5. He writes thus. But the Miltiades to whom he refers has left other monuments of his own zeal for the Divine Scriptures, in the discourses which he composed against the Greeks and against the Jews, answering each of them separately in two books. And in addition he addresses an apology to the earthly rulers, in behalf of the philosophy which he embraced.

CHAPTER EIGHTEEN

The Manner in which Apollonius refuted the Phrygians, and the Persons whom he Mentions

1. AS THE SO-CALLED Phrygian heresy was still flourishing in Phrygia in his time, Apollonius also, an ecclesiastical writer, undertook its refutation, and wrote a special work against it, correcting in detail the

false prophecies current among them and reproving the life of the founders of the heresy. But hear his own words respecting Montanus:

2. **"His actions and his teaching show who this new teacher is. This is he who taught the dissolution of marriage; who made laws for fasting; who named Pepuza and Tymion, small towns in Phrygia, Jerusalem, wishing to gather people to them from all directions; who appointed collectors of money; who contrived the receiving of gifts under the name of offerings; who provided salaries for those who preached his doctrine, that its teaching might prevail through gluttony."**

3. He writes thus concerning Montanus; and a little farther on he writes as follows concerning his prophetesses: **"We show that these first prophetesses themselves, as soon as they were filled with the Spirit, abandoned their**

husbands. How falsely therefore they speak who call **Prisca** a virgin."

4. Afterwards he says: **"Does not all Scripture seem to you to forbid a prophet to receive gifts and money? When therefore I see the prophetess receiving gold and silver and costly garments, how can I avoid reproving her?"**

5. And again a little farther on he speaks thus concerning one of their confessors:

"So also Themiso, who was clothed with plausible covetousness, could not endure the sign of confession, but threw aside bonds for an abundance of possessions. Yet, though he should have been humble on this account, he dared to boast as a martyr, and in imitation of the apostle, he wrote a certain catholic epistle, to instruct those whose faith was better than his own, contending for words of empty sound, and blaspheming against the Lord and the apostles and the

holy Church."

6. And again concerning others of those honored among them as martyrs, he writes as follows:

Not to speak of many, let the prophetess herself tell us of Alexander, who called himself a martyr, with whom she is in the habit of banqueting, and who is worshipped by many. We need not mention his robberies and other daring deeds for which he was punished, but the archives contain them.

7. Which of these forgives the sins of the other? Does the prophet the robberies of the martyr, or the martyr the covetousness of the prophet? For although the Lord said, 'Provide neither gold, nor silver, neither two coats,' Matthew 10:9-10 these men, in complete opposition, transgress in respect to the possession of the forbidden things. For we will show that those whom they call prophets and martyrs gather their gain not only from rich men, but also from the poor, and orphans, and widows.

8. But if they are confident, let them stand up and discuss these matters, that if convicted they may hereafter cease transgressing. For the fruits of the prophet must be tried; 'for the tree is known by its fruit.' Matthew 12:33

9. But that those who wish may know concerning Alexander, he was tried by Æmilius Frontinus, proconsul at Ephesus; not on account of the Name, but for the robberies which he had committed, being already an apostate. Afterwards, having falsely declared for the name of the Lord, he was released, having deceived the faithful that were there. And his own parish, from which he came, did not receive him, because he was a robber. Those who wish to learn about him have the public records of Asia. And yet the prophet with whom he spent many years knows nothing about him!

10. Exposing him, through him we expose also the pretense of the prophet. We could show the same thing of many others. But if

they are confident, let them endure the test.

11. Again, in another part of his work he speaks as follows of the prophets of whom they boast:

"If they deny that their prophets have received gifts, let them acknowledge this: that if they are convicted of receiving them, they are not prophets. And we will bring a multitude of proofs of this. But it is necessary that all the fruits of a prophet should be examined. Tell me, does a prophet dye his hair? Does a prophet stain his eyelids? Does a prophet delight in adornment? Does a prophet play with tables and dice? Does a prophet lend on usury? Let them confess whether these things are lawful or not; but I will show that they have been done by them."

12. This same Apollonius states in the same work that, at the time of his writing, it was the fortieth year since Montanus had begun his pretended prophecy.

13. And he says also that Zoticus, who

was mentioned by the former writer, when Maximilla was pretending to prophesy in Pepuza, resisted her and endeavored to refute the spirit that was working in her; but was prevented by those who agreed with her. He mentions also a certain Thraseas among the martyrs of that time.

He speaks, moreover, of a tradition that the Saviour commanded his apostles not to depart from Jerusalem for twelve years. He uses testimonies also from the Revelation of John, and he relates that a dead man had, through the Divine power, been raised by John himself in Ephesus. He also adds other things by which he fully and abundantly exposes the error of the heresy of which we have been speaking. These are the matters recorded by Apollonius.

CHAPTER NINETEEN

Serapion on the Heresy of the Phrygians

1. SERAPION, WHO, AS report says, succeeded Maximinus at that time as bishop of the church of Antioch, mentions the works of Apolinarius against the above-mentioned heresy. And he alludes to him in a private letter to Caricus and Pontius, in which he himself exposes the same heresy, and adds the following words:

578

2. **"That you may see that the doings of this lying band of the new prophecy, so called, are an abomination to all the brotherhood throughout the world, I have sent you writings of the most blessed Claudius Apolinarius, bishop of Hierapolis in Asia."**

3. In the same letter of Serapion the signatures of several bishops are found, one of whom subscribes himself as follows:

"I, Aurelius Cyrenius, a witness, pray for your health."

And another in this manner:

"Ælius Publius Julius, bishop of Debeltum, a colony of Thrace. As God lives in the heavens, the blessed Sotas in Anchialus desired to cast the demon out of Priscilla, but the hypocrites did not permit him."

4. And the autograph signatures of many other bishops who agreed with them are contained in the same letter.

So much for these persons.

CHAPTER TWENTY

The Writings of Irenæus against the Schismatics at Rome

1. IRENÆUS WROTE SEVERAL letters against those who were disturbing the sound ordinance of the Church at Rome. One of them was to Blastus On Schism; another to Florinus On Monarchy, or That God is not the Author of Evil. For Florinus

580

seemed to be defending this opinion. And because he was being drawn away by the error of Valentinus, Irenæus wrote his work On the Ogdoad, in which he shows that he himself had been acquainted with the first successors of the apostles.

2. At the close of the treatise we have found a most beautiful note which we are constrained to insert in this work. It runs as follows:

"I adjure you who may copy this book, by our Lord Jesus Christ, and by his glorious advent when he comes to judge the living and the dead, to compare what you shall write, and correct it carefully by this manuscript, and also to write this adjuration, and place it in the copy."

3. These things may be profitably read in his work, and related by us, that we may have those ancient and truly holy men as the best example of painstaking carefulness.

4. In the letter to Florinus, of which we have spoken, Irenæus mentions again his

intimacy with Polycarp, saying:

These doctrines, O Florinus, to speak mildly, are not of sound judgment. These doctrines disagree with the Church, and drive into the greatest impiety those who accept them. These doctrines, not even the heretics outside of the Church, have ever dared to publish. These doctrines, the presbyters who were before us, and who were companions of the apostles, did not deliver to you.

5. For when I was a boy, I saw you in lower Asia with Polycarp, moving in splendor in the royal court, and endeavoring to gain his approbation.

6. I remember the events of that time more clearly than those of recent years. For what boys learn, growing with their mind, becomes joined with it; so that I am able to describe the very place in which the blessed Polycarp sat as he discoursed, and his goings out and his comings in, and the manner of his life, and his physical appearance, and his discourses

to the people, and the accounts which he gave of his intercourse with John and with the others who had seen the Lord. And as he remembered their words, and what he heard from them concerning the Lord, and concerning his miracles and his teaching, having received them from eyewitnesses of the 'Word of life,' 1 John 1:1 Polycarp related all things in harmony with the Scriptures.

7. These things being told me by the mercy of God, I listened to them attentively, noting them down, not on paper, but in my heart. And continually, through God's grace, I recall them faithfully. And I am able to bear witness before God that if that blessed and apostolic presbyter had heard any such thing, he would have cried out, and stopped his ears, and as was his custom, would have exclaimed, O good God, unto what times have you spared me that I should endure these things? And he would have fled from the place where, sitting or standing, he had heard such words.

8. And this can be shown plainly from the letters which he sent, either to the neighboring churches for their confirmation, or to some of the brethren, admonishing and exhorting them. Thus far Irenæus.

CHAPTER TWENTY ONE

How Appolonius suffered Martyrdom at Rome

1. ABOUT THE SAME TIME, in the reign of Commodus, our condition became more favorable, and through the grace of God the churches throughout the entire world enjoyed peace, and the word of salvation was leading every soul, from every race of man to the devout worship of the God of the universe. So that now at Rome many who

were highly distinguished for wealth and family turned with all their household and relatives unto their salvation.

2. But the demon who hates what is good, being malignant in his nature, could not endure this, but prepared himself again for conflict, contriving many devices against us. And he brought to the judgment seat Apollonius, of the city of Rome, a man renowned among the faithful for learning and philosophy, having stirred up one of his servants, who was well fitted for such a purpose, to accuse him.

3. But this wretched man made the charge unseasonably, because by a royal decree it was unlawful that informers of such things should live. And his legs were broken immediately, Perennius the judge having pronounced this sentence upon him.

4. But the martyr, highly beloved of God, being earnestly entreated and requested by the judge to give an account of himself before the Senate, made in the presence

of all an eloquent defense of the faith for which he was witnessing. And as if by decree of the Senate he was put to death by decapitation; an ancient law requiring that those who were brought to the judgment seat and refused to recant should not be liberated. Whoever desires to know his arguments before the judge and his answers to the questions of Perennius, and his entire defense before the Senate will find them in the records of the ancient martyrdoms which we have collected.

CHAPTER TWENTY TWO

The Bishops that were well known at this Time

IN THE TENTH YEAR of the reign of Commodus, Victor succeeded Eleutherus, the latter having held the episcopate for thirteen years. In the same year, after Julian had completed his tenth year, Demetrius received the charge of the parishes at Alexandria. At this time the above-mentioned Serapion, the eighth from the apostles, was still well known as bishop of the church at Antioch. Theophilus presided at Cæsarea in Palestine; and Narcissus, whom we have mentioned before, still had charge of the church at Jerusalem. Bacchylus at the same time was bishop of Corinth in Greece, and Polycrates of the parish of Ephesus. And besides these a multitude of others, as is likely, were then prominent. But we have given the names of those alone, the soundness of whose faith has come down to us in writing.

CHAPTER TWENTY THREE

The Question then agitated concerning the Passover

1. A QUESTION OF NO small importance arose at that time. For the parishes of all Asia, as from an older tradition, held that the fourteenth day of the moon, on which day the Jews were commanded to sacrifice the lamb, should be observed as the feast of the Saviour's passover. It was therefore necessary to end their fast on

that day, whatever day of the week it should happen to be. But it was not the custom of the churches in the rest of the world to end it at this time, as they observed the practice which, from apostolic tradition, has prevailed to the present time, of terminating the fast on no other day than on that of the resurrection of our Saviour.

2. Synods and assemblies of bishops were held on this account, and all, with one consent, through mutual correspondence drew up an ecclesiastical decree, that the mystery of the resurrection of the Lord should be celebrated on no other but the Lord's day, and that we should observe the close of the paschal fast on this day only. There is still extant a writing of those who were then assembled in Palestine, over whom Theophilus, bishop of Cæsarea, and Narcissus, bishop of Jerusalem, presided. And there is also another writing extant of those who were assembled at Rome to consider the same question, which bears

the name of Bishop Victor; also of the bishops in Pontus over whom Palmas, as the oldest, presided; and of the parishes in Gaul of which Irenæus was bishop, and of those in Osrhoëne and the cities there; and a personal letter of Bacchylus, bishop of the church at Corinth, and of a great many others, who uttered the same opinion and judgment, and cast the same vote.

3. And that which has been given above was their unanimous decision.

CHAPTER TWENTY FOUR
The Disagreement in Asia

1. BUT THE BISHOPS OF Asia, led by Polycrates, decided to hold to the old custom handed down to them. He himself, in a letter which he addressed to Victor and the church of Rome, set forth in the following words the tradition which had come down to him:

2. We observe the exact day; neither adding, nor taking away. For in Asia also

great lights have fallen asleep, which shall rise again on the day of the Lord's coming, when he shall come with glory from heaven, and shall seek out all the saints. Among these are Philip, one of the twelve apostles, who fell asleep in Hierapolis; and his two aged virgin daughters, and another daughter, who lived in the Holy Spirit and now rests at Ephesus; and, moreover, John, who was both a witness and a teacher, who reclined upon the bosom of the Lord, and, being a priest, wore the sacerdotal plate.

3. He fell asleep at Ephesus.

4. And Polycarp in Smyrna, who was a bishop and martyr; and Thraseas, bishop and martyr from Eumenia, who fell asleep in Smyrna.

5. Why need I mention the bishop and martyr Sagaris who fell asleep in Laodicea, or the blessed Papirius, or Melito, the Eunuch who lived altogether in the Holy Spirit, and who lies in Sardis, awaiting the episcopate from heaven, when he shall rise

from the dead?

6. All these observed the fourteenth day of the passover according to the Gospel, deviating in no respect, but following the rule of faith. And I also, Polycrates, the least of you all, do according to the tradition of my relatives, some of whom I have closely followed. For seven of my relatives were bishops; and I am the eighth. And my relatives always observed the day when the people put away the leaven.

7. I, therefore, brethren, who have lived sixty-five years in the Lord, and have met with the brethren throughout the world, and have gone through every Holy Scripture, am not affrighted by terrifying words. For those greater than I have said 'We ought to obey God rather than man.' Acts 5:29

8. He then writes of all the bishops who were present with him and thought as he did. His words are as follows:

"I could mention the bishops who were present, whom I summoned at your

desire; whose names, should I write them, would constitute a great multitude. And they, beholding my littleness, gave their consent to the letter, knowing that I did not bear my gray hairs in vain, but had always governed my life by the Lord Jesus."

9. Thereupon Victor, who presided over the church at Rome, immediately attempted to cut off from the common unity the parishes of all Asia, with the churches that agreed with them, as heterodox; and he wrote letters and declared all the brethren there wholly excommunicate.

10. But this did not please all the bishops. And they besought him to consider the things of peace, and of neighborly unity and love. Words of theirs are extant, sharply rebuking Victor.

11. Among them was Irenæus, who, sending letters in the name of the brethren in Gaul over whom he presided, maintained that the mystery of the resurrection of the Lord

should be observed only on the Lord's day. He fittingly admonishes Victor that he should not cut off whole churches of God which observed the tradition of an ancient custom and after many other words he proceeds as follows:

12. For the controversy is not only concerning the day, but also concerning the very manner of the fast. For some think that they should fast one day, others two, yet others more; some, moreover, count their day as consisting of forty hours day and night.

13. And this variety in its observance has not originated in our time; but long before in that of our ancestors. It is likely that they did not hold to strict accuracy, and thus formed a custom for their posterity according to their own simplicity and peculiar mode. Yet all of these lived none the less in peace, and we also live in peace with one another; and the disagreement in regard to the fast confirms the agreement in the faith.

14. He adds to this the following account, which I may properly insert:

Among these were the presbyters before Soter, who presided over the church which you now rule. We mean Anicetus, and Pius, and Hyginus, and Telesphorus, and Xystus. They neither observed it themselves, nor did they permit those after them to do so. And yet though not observing it, they were none the less at peace with those who came to them from the parishes in which it was observed; although this observance was more opposed to those who did not observe it.

15. But none were ever cast out on account of this form; but the presbyters before you who did not observe it, sent the eucharist to those of other parishes who observed it.

16. And when the blessed Polycarp was at Rome in the time of Anicetus, and they disagreed a little about certain other things, they immediately made peace with one another, not caring to quarrel over this matter. For neither could Anicetus persuade

Polycarp not to observe what he had always observed with John the disciple of our Lord, and the other apostles with whom he had associated; neither could Polycarp persuade Anicetus to observe it as he said that he ought to follow the customs of the presbyters that had preceded him.

17. But though matters were in this shape, they communed together, and Anicetus conceded the administration of the eucharist in the church to Polycarp, manifestly as a mark of respect. And they parted from each other in peace, both those who observed, and those who did not, maintaining the peace of the whole church.

18. Thus Irenæus, who truly was well named, became a peacemaker in this matter, exhorting and negotiating in this way in behalf of the peace of the churches. And he conferred by letter about this mooted question, not only with Victor, but also with most of the other rulers of the churches.

CHAPTER TWENTY FIVE

How All came to an Agreement
respecting the Passover

1. THOSE IN PALESTINE WHOM we have recently mentioned, Narcissus and Theophilus, and with them Cassius, bishop of the church of Tyre, and Clarus of the church of Ptolemais, and those who met with them, having stated many things respecting the tradition concerning the passover which had come to them in succession from the

apostles, at the close of their writing add these words:

2. **"Endeavor to send copies of our letter to every church, that we may not furnish occasion to those who easily deceive their souls. We show you indeed that also in Alexandria they keep it on the same day that we do. For letters are carried from us to them and from them to us, so that in the same manner and at the same time we keep the sacred day."**

CHAPTER TWENTY SIX

The Elegant Works of Irenæus which have come down to us

BESIDES THE WORKS AND letters of Irenæus which we have mentioned, a certain book of his On Knowledge, written against the Greeks, very concise and remarkably forcible, is extant; and another, which he dedicated to a brother Marcian, In Demonstration of the Apostolic Preaching; and a volume containing various

Dissertations, in which he mentions the Epistle to the Hebrews and the so-called Wisdom of Solomon, making quotations from them. These are the works of Irenæus which have come to our knowledge.

Commodus having ended his reign after thirteen years, Severus became emperor in less than six months after his death, Pertinax having reigned during the intervening time.

CHAPTER TWENTY SEVEN

The Works of Others that flourished at that Time

NUMEROUS MEMORIALS OF THE faithful zeal of the ancient ecclesiastical men of that time are still preserved by many. Of these we would note particularly the writings of Heraclitus On the Apostle, and those of Maximus on the question so much discussed among heretics, the Origin of Evil, and on the Creation of Matter. Also those of Candidus on the Hexæmeron, and of Apion on the same subject; likewise of Sextus on the Resurrection, and another treatise of Arabianus, and writings of a multitude of others, in regard to whom, because we have no data, it is impossible to state in our work when they lived, or to give any account of their history. And works of many others have come down to us whose names we are unable to give, orthodox and ecclesiastical, as their interpretations of the Divine Scriptures show, but unknown to us, because their names are not stated in their writings.

CHAPTER TWENTY EIGHT

Those who first advanced the Heresy of Artemon; their Manner of Life, and how they dared to corrupt the Sacred Scriptures

1. IN A LABORIOUS WORK by one of these writers against the heresy of Artemon, which Paul of Samosata attempted to revive again in our day, there is an account

appropriate to the history which we are now examining.

2. For he criticises, as a late innovation, the above-mentioned heresy which teaches that the Saviour was a mere man, because they were attempting to magnify it as ancient. Having given in his work many other arguments in refutation of their blasphemous falsehood, he adds the following words:

3. For they say that all the early teachers and the apostles received and taught what they now declare, and that the truth of the Gospel was preserved until the times of Victor, who was the thirteenth bishop of Rome from Peter, but that from his successor, Zephyrinus, the truth had been corrupted.

4. And what they say might be plausible, if first of all the Divine Scriptures did not contradict them. And there are writings of certain brethren older than the times of Victor, which they wrote in behalf of the truth against the heathen, and against the

heresies which existed in their day. I refer to Justin and Miltiades and Tatian and Clement and many others, in all of whose works Christ is spoken of as God.

5. For who does not know the works of Irenæus and of Melito and of others which teach that Christ is God and man? And how many psalms and hymns, written by the faithful brethren from the beginning, celebrate Christ the Word of God, speaking of him as Divine.

6. How then since the opinion held by the Church has been preached for so many years, can its preaching have been delayed as they affirm, until the times of Victor? And how is it that they are not ashamed to speak thus falsely of Victor, knowing well that he cut off from communion Theodotus, the cobbler, the leader and father of this God-denying apostasy, and the first to declare that Christ is mere man? For if Victor agreed with their opinions, as their slander affirms, how came he to cast out Theodotus, the

inventor of this heresy?

7. So much in regard to Victor. His bishopric lasted ten years, and Zephyrinus was appointed his successor about the ninth year of the reign of Severus. The author of the above-mentioned book, concerning the founder of this heresy, narrates another event which occurred in the time of Zephyrinus, using these words:

8. I will remind many of the brethren of a fact which took place in our time, which, had it happened in Sodom, might, I think, have proved a warning to them. There was a certain confessor, Natalius, not long ago, but in our own day.

9. This man was deceived at one time by Asclepiodotus and another Theodotus, a money-changer. Both of them were disciples of Theodotus, the cobbler, who, as I have said, was the first person excommunicated by Victor, bishop at that time, on account of this sentiment, or rather senselessness.

10. Natalius was persuaded by them to

allow himself to be chosen bishop of this heresy with a salary, to be paid by them, of one hundred and fifty denarii a month.

11. When he had thus connected himself with them, he was warned oftentimes by the Lord through visions. For the compassionate God and our Lord Jesus Christ was not willing that a witness of his own sufferings, being cast out of the Church, should perish.

12. But as he paid little regard to the visions, because he was ensnared by the first position among them and by that shameful covetousness which destroys a great many, he was scourged by holy angels, and punished severely through the entire night. Thereupon having risen in the morning, he put on sackcloth and covered himself with ashes, and with great haste and tears he fell down before Zephyrinus, the bishop, rolling at the feet not only of the clergy, but also of the laity; and he moved with his tears the compassionate

Church of the merciful Christ. And though he used much supplication, and showed the welts of the stripes which he had received, yet scarcely was he taken back into communion.

13. We will add from the same writer some other extracts concerning them, which run as follows:

They have treated the Divine Scriptures recklessly and without fear. They have set aside the rule of ancient faith; and Christ they have not known. They do not endeavor to learn what the Divine Scriptures declare, but strive laboriously after any form of syllogism which may be devised to sustain their impiety. And if any one brings before them a passage of Divine Scripture, they see whether a conjunctive or disjunctive form of syllogism can be made from it.

14. And as being of the earth and speaking of the earth, and as ignorant of him who comes from above, they forsake the holy writings of God to devote themselves to geometry.

Euclid is laboriously measured by some of them; and Aristotle and Theophrastus are admired; and Galen, perhaps, by some is even worshipped.

15. But that those who use the arts of unbelievers for their heretical opinions and adulterate the simple faith of the Divine Scriptures by the craft of the godless, are far from the faith, what need is there to say? Therefore they have laid their hands boldly upon the Divine Scriptures, alleging that they have corrected them.

16. That I am not speaking falsely of them in this matter, whoever wishes may learn. For if any one will collect their respective copies, and compare them one with another, he will find that they differ greatly.

17. Those of Asclepiades, for example, do not agree with those of Theodotus. And many of these can be obtained, because their disciples have assiduously written the corrections, as they call them, that is the corruptions, of each of them. Again, those

of Hermophilus do not agree with these, and those of Apollonides are not consistent with themselves. For you can compare those prepared by them at an earlier date with those which they corrupted later, and you will find them widely different.

18. But how daring this offense is, it is not likely that they themselves are ignorant. For either they do not believe that the Divine Scriptures were spoken by the Holy Spirit, and thus are unbelievers, or else they think themselves wiser than the Holy Spirit, and in that case what else are they than demoniacs? For they cannot deny the commission of the crime, since the copies have been written by their own hands. For they did not receive such Scriptures from their instructors, nor can they produce any copies from which they were transcribed.

19. But some of them have not thought it worth while to corrupt them, but simply deny the law and the prophets, and thus through their lawless and impious teaching under

pretense of grace, have sunk to the lowest depths of perdition.

Let this suffice for these things.

CONTINUES IN VOLUME TWO

GRANDTYPECLASSICS.COM

"There is no friend as loyal as a book." E. Hemingway

A Christmas Carol BY C. DICKENS
A Tale of Two Cities BY C. DICKENS
Alice in Wonderland BY L. CARROLL
Animal Farm BY G. ORWELL
Anna Karenina BY L. TOLSTOY
Anne of Green Gables BY L. M. MONTGOMERY
Black Beauty BY A. SEWELL
Frankenstein BY M. SHELLEY
Gone with the Wind BY M. MITCHELL
Great Expectations BY C. DICKENS
Grimm's Fairy Tales BY J. AND W. GRIMM
In Our Time BY E. HEMINGWAY
Jane Eyre BY C. BRONTË
Les Misérables BY V. HUGO
Little Women BY L. M. ALCOTT
Moby Dick BY H. MELVILLE
Oliver Twist BY C. DICKENS
Peter Pan BY J. M. BARRIE
Pride & Prejudice BY J. AUSTEN
Robinson Crusoe BY D. DEFOE
The Art of War BY S. TZU
The Count of Monte Cristo BY A. DUMAS
And Many More...

www.ingramcontent.com/pod-product-compliance
Lightning Source LLC
Chambersburg PA
CBHW030805100426
42814CB00019B/438/J